the
BEST
is yet to
COME

"Sr. Anne Bryan Smollin was one of the most joyful and effective communicators of the Gospel that I have ever met. She was a force of nature—and of joy. Renowned for her stories, celebrated for her wit, and beloved for her warmth, she was also a terrific writer. Her new book is a heartfelt reminder to seek holiness in the everyday and joy in every moment."

Rev. James Martin, S.J.
Author of *Jesus: A Pilgrimage*

"An opportunity to soften our soul, share a bit of laughter, experience a sacred moment, and change our mood for the better—*The Best Is Yet to Come* is classic Sr. Anne Bryan Smollin and a true spiritual tonic for regaining a healthier perspective in today's stressful, sometimes anxious world."

Robert J. Wicks
Author of *Riding the Dragon*

"The cycle of life is a series of endings and beginnings, and each change brings its own gift. Yes, we grieve the loss of an amazing woman—Sr. Anne Bryan Smollin—yet still we rejoice that her vision and passion for sharing joy, laughter, humor, and spirituality are now made accessible to us in her final inspiring and spirit-filled book, *The Best Is Yet to Come*. This tapestry of reflections and stories woven so beautifully invite us to live fully, to seize life, and to discover God within the ordinariness of daily life—a God who often hides in the surprise and wonder of beauty and blessing around us. Anne's nurturing words of wisdom frequently spoken at the LA Religious Education Congress and at many other national and international events will now reach the minds and hearts of so many more of God's people who long for words of hope and encouragement. What a precious collection of reflections, bubbling over with the energy and grace of one who prayed, 'Please, God, help me to touch one person.'"

Edith Prendergast, R.S.C.
Former Director of Religious Education
Archdiocese of Los Angeles

the BEST *is yet to* COME

LIVING FULLY IN EACH MOMENT

Anne Bryan Smollin

SORIN BOOKS · Notre Dame, Indiana

www.sorinbooks.com

Paperback: ISBN-13 978-1-933495-96-5

E-book: ISBN-13 978-1-933495-97-2

Cover and text design by Katherine J. Ross.

Interior images "300 People Silhouettes" vectors by Vector Open Stock.

Printed and bound in the United States of America.

Library of Congress Cataloging-in-Publication Data
Names: Smollin, Anne Bryan, author.
Title: The best is yet to come : living fully in each moment / Anne Bryan Smollin, C.S.J.
Description: Notre Dame, Indiana : Sorin Books, 2016. | Includes bibliographical references and index.
Identifiers: LCCN 2016017984 (print) | LCCN 2016031267 (ebook) | ISBN 9781933495965 (alk. paper) | ISBN 1933495960 (alk. paper) | ISBN 9781933495972 () | ISBN 1933495979 ()
Subjects: LCSH: Meditations.
Classification: LCC BV4832.3 .S6525 2016 (print) | LCC BV4832.3 (ebook) | DDC 242--dc23
LC record available at https://lccn.loc.gov/2016017984

In celebration of this,
my fiftieth jubilee year as a Sister of St. Joseph of Carondelet,
and in thanksgiving for this blessing,
I dedicate this book to my mother, Irma,
my sister, Mary Kay,
my local C.S.J. community, and my best friend, Patricia.
You are always there for me,
supportive, loving, and life giving.
I also dedicate this book to my friends:
Janet, Rose Ann, Cyril,
and to all those Sisters of St. Joseph
who have walked these years with me in friendship.
I have been abundantly blessed by your presence in my life.
I offer deep gratitude.
Thank you.

CONTENTS

Foreword

BY
SISTER PATRICIA
A. ST. JOHN, C.S.J.

A woman left clear directions about her final wishes upon her death. Among her requests was the directive, "Please bury me with a fork in my hand." When asked about the curious request, the woman's husband responded that his wife had attended numerous potluck dinners at her church. Having completed the main course, participants were always asked to keep their forks while dishes and other utensils were

collected and cleaned. The reason? Dessert had not yet been served; the best was yet to come.

This story was intended for the start of the last chapter as outlined by Sr. Anne, titled "The Best Is Yet to Come." While she left no notes for that chapter, she has told the story associated with the title before.

Sr. Anne Bryan Smollin died peacefully but unexpectedly on September 25, 2014, in her home in Albany, New York. I was with her. We shared communal life as Sisters of St. Joseph for thirty years; we were best friends and soul mates. While the exact cause of her death is unknown, we do know that Anne left this world as she participated in it, as swiftly and surprisingly as a bolt of lightning.

The one thing of which we can be sure is that Anne's work was not done. For so many, she offered a listening ear, a helping hand, and an encouraging word. Small acts of kindness and encouragement touched others. She formed bonds of affection with the young pregnant teens at Catholic Charities' Community Maternity Services, not only through group therapy sessions but also as they assisted with various clerical duties at Counseling for Laity where Anne was executive director. As she passed by them as they worked, she would spontaneously challenge them:

"Tell me three things you like about yourself," simultaneously getting to know the young women as well as bringing their best qualities to mind. There were also larger gestures of generosity such as delivering the fixings for a complete Thanksgiving dinner to a former student whose family had fallen on hard times. Many years before, when he thought he couldn't attend his graduation because he didn't have anything proper to wear, Anne took him shopping for a suit. He never forgot her care and reached out to Anne again, knowing he could count on her.

Reflecting back in broad strokes over the last five decades—the 1960s when Anne ministered among the poor in Albany with Fr. Hubbard (later Bishop Hubbard of the Albany Diocese); the '70s when she assisted families through Parent Effectiveness Training; the '80s spent serving on the board for the AIDS Council of Northeastern New York (now the Alliance for Positive Health); the '90s when she led the Albany Rotary as its first woman president, celebrating service above self; in these millennial years when she contributed so proudly to the College of St. Rose community as a member of the board of trustees; and all this in addition to her full-time ministry as psychologist as well as maintaining a full circuit of speaking engagements in the United States, Canada, Europe, and Australia—I don't think I can ever recall Anne saying no to anyone at any time. Her wide-open heart was available to anybody in need, including for counseling services without remuneration. Sometimes the recipients of her kindness weren't even aware of all she was doing for them.

Several years ago, having lived with Anne for a few years, I had gotten off the phone after a long conversation with a friend in need. I shared with Anne that I was really concerned about this person; she was receiving counseling twice a week. "Isn't that heavy-duty counseling?" I asked Anne. Without skipping a beat, she responded, "Patti, you needed residential treatment; you had to move in!"

The enabling foundation for Anne's life was her beloved community, the Sisters of St. Joseph. This was the motivation behind her generous heart and joyous spirit, this is what drove her pursuit of excellence in all its forms, and this is what impassioned her to help others grow toward wholeness and holiness.

At once she could be a soothing balm and a messenger of joy, easing our pain and celebrating our achievements. Anne was equally at ease with public officials and guests at the soup kitchen. She could talk policy or poetry. Her presence was both larger than life and intimately attentive. She helped us laugh at ourselves and at our humanity, and Anne challenged us to put the absurdities of life into a healthy perspective.

Whether she was addressing a handful of parishioners at a communion breakfast or inspiring thousands of participants in the arena at the Los Angeles Congress, her prayer was the same: "God, please help me to touch one person's life." That's how focused she was, too, if you were engaged in a conversation with her, as she often asked, "Tell me what's going for you?" It was as if no one else existed for that moment, only you.

Many folks have commented to me that life must have been hilarious living with Anne and that, undoubtedly, we never stopped laughing. Actually, Anne was quite different at home. We created a space together that was marked by a generous spirit of hospitality. We delighted in the ordinary events of our life and made them sacred. We enjoyed quiet dinners, the company of good friends, and simple pleasures such as sitting in the backyard during warm summer nights and watching the sun go down, fun-loving Uno games where once again she would be declared the Uno champ, or mindless evenings watching silly sitcoms. I didn't expect her to entertain me, although she often made me laugh at myself and helped me to find the lighter side of life. Every Christmas season, we actually did watch *Rudolph, the Red-Nosed Reindeer*, as well as *It's a Wonderful Life*.

While she joked about wanting to drive a Lincoln, Anne was more like a horse and buggy in her simplicity. She was easy to *be with*. She could equally enjoy an elegant dinner out or a pizza at home. Anne appreciated so many little things, but most of all, she delighted in coming home after work, taking a shower to wash away the stress of the day, putting on her pajamas regardless of the time, and relaxing in her chair. That said, she had a childlike joy that welcomed adventure; one summer night, I asked if she wanted to go to Ross's for a coffee ice-cream cone. Already in her pajamas, she exclaimed, "Great idea!" Off we went. As she sat in the car eating her favorite flavor of ice cream, she said, "Patti, this is the best idea you've ever had!" (I could always count on her astute assessment and honest feedback in any situation!)

Carefully woven throughout our life together were transparent conversations that were often focused on our blessings: our home, our friendship, our community, our families, our opportunities, and the many intersections of our work that broadened our circle of friends. We were careful not to take it all for granted, neither our friendship nor our life together and all that it entailed. She would urge you to do the same and to take time to enjoy the people, places, and things that are important to you.

A lover of photography, Anne delighted in every opportunity to browse through the International Center for Photography in New York City. She would often go off on an adventure to seek photo opportunities, taking long drives through wooded areas with her camera or walking through a park to find just the right light and shadow, playing with f-stop, aperture, and angle. During a winter storm, when everyone was urged to stay off the roads, she would bundle up and walk the neighborhood to capture the snow-laden branches of tree-lined streets. She would be quick to capture the unfurling of the rose petals on the bushes in our backyard, carefully and patiently waiting until just the right moment.

Second only to our backyard, Anne's favorite place to spend time was on Massachusetts' distinct peninsula, Cape Cod. Each year we would make at least one pilgrimage to its sandy shores and mountainous dunes, taking delight in its beauty, salty air, and relaxed ambiance as if seeing it all for the first time. It was sacred.

On our way, we had a special ritual: "Tell me three things you love about me. Now tell me what I do that drives you crazy, and yes, you must limit it to three." This conversation kept our life authentic, honest, loving, and deeply caring. It made our communal life strong, solid, and sustaining. We served as mirrors for each other, reflecting back what we saw and challenging each other to see God's face mirrored in and with those we serve.

Through our life in community as Sisters of St. Joseph, Anne and I shared a passionate commitment to the mission of Jesus, believing that all of our efforts should be directed toward those core values of co-creating God's reign of peace and justice among us. Simply put, we believed we could make the world a better place, changing it through our interactions and our relationships, one person at a time. It didn't matter what you did but *how* you did it.

Life at home then was a place where she could be herself. It was a safe place. There were no hidden agendas, no expectations, and no demands. She loved what we Sisters of St. Joseph call our "local" community: the life we celebrated, the prayers we shared, and the rituals we created together. Thus, our communal life provided a place and a space to recuperate, to restore, and to rejuvenate so that each day we could awaken and start all over again, giving everything we had to a world in need. This was the gift of our life together as Sisters of St. Joseph and the heart of our friendship: to be of service to others and to keep inviting them into relationship.

One week before Anne died, we enjoyed a wonderful evening with Benedictine sister Joan Chittister. Anne and I, together with Joan and her companion, Sister Maureen, had gone out to dinner the night before Joan's lecture on "The Prophetic Call." Here is the last story Anne wrote, jotting it on the legal-size paper she always used, dating it, and placing it in the folder with the manuscript for this book the day before she died:

> There's nothing like a visit with an old friend. It's as if you had been together the day before. You just pick up where you left off the last time and enjoy the moment. You find the wonderful connections

that have been a part of the friendship you have shared for years.

Joan Chittister was giving a lecture here in Albany, and it gave us the chance to be together. Joan, Maureen, Patti, and I had a wonderful dinner together the first night. I wanted Patti to meet Maureen, who is as "good as gold," and I knew that Joan would enjoy seeing Patti again and that Patti would be energized by the interaction and conversation. I love it when my friends appreciate and nourish each other. We need others to help us grow into wholeness, to lift us up, to encourage us, and to challenge us to live fully. And, reciprocally, we need to do that for others.

We had a great time! Joan and I had two days of "catching up" and "looking forward," just sharing where and what we had been through since our last visit.

Joan has a bird, a beautiful parakeet that traveled with her and Maureen from Erie, Pennsylvania. Apparently, the bird talks incessantly once she knows you. However, this was our first meeting, and the bird never uttered a sound in front of me for two days. Joan decided that she wanted the parakeet and me to be friends. She brought the bird over to me and told me to hold out my finger. I did as she instructed, and Joan placed the bird on my finger. The parakeet proceeded to bite my hand! I am sure I scared the poor little thing with my loud scream and perhaps ended the possibility of any relationship we might have had, but Joan wanted the parakeet to apologize and kept bringing the bird over to me.

My visit with Joan was life giving. It's wonderful when we have the opportunity to introduce friends to other friends and cross-pollinate these relationships across contexts. It broadens our circle and widens our world. As a blessing for each other, our lives are enriched and we are gifted with joy. But I'm afraid I will never be friends with Joan's parakeet.

Anne used to tell me, "We never know what another person is carrying in their heart: what sorrow, pain, discouragement, devastation. Let's always err on the side of kindness, Patti." I think Anne would impart these words for us today. In her spirit, heed them. Cynicism is a poison that stifles possibility; believe, as she did, that you *can* make the world a better place. Change it, not so much by what you do but by *how* you do it. And always, always, err on the side of kindness.

Anne chaired a community meeting the night before she died. In her notes she wrote, "We are all in this together; be kind to each other; stay positive." In addition to the signature tag line with which Anne ended all of her lectures—Live well, love much, laugh often—this is a wonderful mantra with which to remember her and the message of this final book: to live each moment fully, to discover the sacred in the ordinary, and to find joy and happiness through the people and events of our daily interactions. Up to her last minute, Anne never wasted any one of her 86,400 seconds. For that, we have all been richly blessed. Let us offer deep gratitude for and find great joy in that gift.

We are consoled in our faith; her permeating spirit is still with us. She has gone to the other side where, with the communion of saints, she continues to intervene, inspire, and ignite a passion for life. She lived as she professed, striving to seize each moment and live it fully, to experience the ordinary events of life as sacramental, and to celebrate possibility. Through her presence and her stories—with her unforgettable pace, impeccable timing, and unpretentious humor catching us off guard and laughing at ourselves—she urged us to do the same.

We trust in God's merciful love and in the promise of fullness of life. We know that for Sister Anne, the best has finally come. May she now celebrate eternal joy and rest peacefully from the work of her hands and the intensity of her heart.

Introduction

Winter is beginning to leave us here in the Northeast. Buds are appearing and the trees are dotted with the soft green of spring; the weeping willow wears a veil of yellow. The forsythia branches are popping with golden jewels, and the crocus and violets are pushing through the earth, announcing their place in the order of things as we herald in springtime. Soon we will be treated to a lovely blanket of flowers. As the seasons change with the passing of another year, we reflect on our own lives. We, too, are always changing. Each day we grow one day older. With the passing of each year, we go places, meet people, and experience events that perhaps we could never imagine. Friends, old and new, move in and out of the seasons of our life. One

thing for which we all long is to live more fully, to live
our lives with a spirit of joy and peace, to experience
the happiness that God desires for us.

There is a story of a motivational speaker who
invited three participants to join him on stage. One
was a lawyer, one a nurse, and the third a mechanic.
The inspiring guru asked them all the same question:
"When you die and people come to your wake, what
do you hope you will hear them say?" The lawyer
spoke first. "I hope I would hear them say I was a fair
and just lawyer and that I took good care of my clients
and represented them as well as possible." The nurse
spoke next. "I hope I would hear them say that I was
a caring, sensitive nurse and that I was compassion-
ate and gave each patient the best care possible. I also
hope I would hear that I was a good mother and that
I raised my children to be good, responsible people.
And I hope I would hear them say I was always there
for them." The mechanic spoke last. "Well, if I die and
people came to my wake I sure hope I would hear
someone say, 'Hey, I think he's still breathing.'"

Basically, we all choose life; we want to live. It is so
important to look at *how* to live rich, full, and whole
lives. We hold on to life-giving moments and create
memories that can help us deal with stressful events.
We pray for good health for ourselves and for those
whom we love. We try to make life easier for our loved
ones and prevent them from experiencing any hurt or
pain. Most of us would admit that we want to live a

long, healthy, full life, and we desire that for our family members and friends as well.

There is a wonderful story about a man in prison who was given the death penalty. He spent many years in the prison cell waiting for the time that eventually would come. The guards were fond of the man. He was easygoing and very friendly. He never caused any trouble, he was helpful to many of the other inmates, and he had a great sense of humor. The fearful day finally arrived. The guards told him that they would like to give him one last request. They said that because he loved to sing and had a great voice they would allow him to sing any song of his choice all the way through from beginning to the end before they took him from his cell. The man was grateful for this last gift.

"So, what is the song you would like to sing?" the prison guard asked.

The prisoner responded, "I would like to sing 'One Billion Bottles of Beer on the Wall.'"

Now don't you wonder how long it would take him to sing that song in its entirety? Would the guards be true to their word and let him sing the complete song? One thing for sure is that it would have lengthened his life. You see, everyone wants to live!

Whether we outwit death through clever requests or are just having fun, we make choices to be more "alive." As we connect with others, laugh and smile, and just "be," we find ourselves more tuned in to the moment. We focus on now, are fully present to that second, and find joy and energy to live that moment fully. Our relationships are enriched; our awareness level is expanded. We "see" what is in front of us; we "hear" the sounds around us. We "feel" connected to the very earth on which we are standing. Each minute is a gift. All that it contains has the potential to feed our hearts and souls.

It is my hope that, as you read through these pages, you will be energized and challenged to make each day count. Each day is such a precious gift. It holds so many magical moments and unsuspecting surprises. Each day carries the potential that allows us to grow more into the people we were born to be, the people God imagined us to be. The choice is ours, minute by minute.

Daily we are challenged with the responsibility to take care of ourselves physically, mentally, emotionally, and spiritually. We need to play and pray, learn and grow. We need to laugh and be positive. In fact, caring for something or someone outside of yourself and having a purpose beyond fulfillment of your immediate needs creates contentment. Contemporary research shows that happy people are more helpful, creative, altruistic, resilient, productive, and likable. They are more interested in others. In short, they are friendlier, healthier people.

Our blessings are so often found in day-to-day events and exchanges. We are blessed by people who touch our ordinary lives, by family members, young and old, who gift us each day. We are touched by our coworkers and blessed by strangers who simply acknowledge our presence by making eye contact as they cross our paths or sharing a smile, thereby sending positive energy our way. Many times these gifts go unnoticed and unappreciated because they are not packaged the way we anticipate or expect them to be.

As you read through these pages, my hope and prayer is that the stories touch your heart and soothe your soul, thus expanding your wide, wonderful world. May we all grow together as we travel this journey of life. May we enrich one another and call forth wholeness and holiness in our everyday relations and interactions.

1

MAKING *Each* *Moment* COUNT

I received an e-mail titled "Something to Think About." It offered an imaginary reflection that I found profound. Let me share my version of this story with you.

There is a national contest that offers as a prize a personal deposit of $86,400 into your private bank account each day for you to use as you wish. However, there is a set of rules attached to the prize.

The first rule is that "everything that you didn't spend each day would be taken away from you. You are the only one who can spend the money. You cannot transfer money into some other account." So, each morning you wake up, the bank opens your account with another $86,400 for that day only.

The second rule is "the bank can end the game without warning. It can close the account and you will not receive a new one." Think about this. What would you do? My guess is that you would spend this money care free, perhaps buying everything and anything you wanted. You would fulfill not only your own needs and desires but also those of special people in your life: your family and friends, all the people you hold dear. You would probably give money to some worthy causes such as Alzheimer's, ALS, cancer, and coronary research to assist with ending these diseases and associative illnesses. Ultimately, I imagine you would find yourself giving money to people you don't even know because $86,400 a day is a lot of money to spend.

What we need to realize is that this game is in fact reality. Each of us has this magical bank account offered to us daily. It is just not something of which we are aware; we cannot see it. This bank is really time. Each morning, we wake up and receive 86,400 seconds as a gift. When we go to bed at night, any of those seconds that we did not use or that we wasted are lost; they are not credited to us. Any time that we haven't lived that day is lost forever.

However, every morning the account is refilled. It is up to you to decide how to spend those seconds. And the account can be taken away from you at any moment without warning.

It is up to you to decide how to live, how to spend those precious 86,400 seconds. We need to take care of ourselves and enjoy life. We need to spend some of those seconds on people we love. We need to spend some of the 86,400 seconds making a difference in our world and in the lives of others, living fully, open to surprises, and celebrating the sacredness of ordinary daily interactions and events.

There are two kinds of people in the world: those who wake up in the morning and say, "Good morning, Lord," and those who wake up in the morning and say, "Good Lord, it's morning!" How we wake up each day and how we spend our precious 86,400 seconds is our choice.

There are some people who hold onto negative moments, who go through life whining. Some people even like being sick so they can complain about it. Think of the seconds, minutes, and even hours that are being wasted and are lost forever. These people are forfeiting the potential of living each moment and seizing every minute.

The late Indian Jesuit and spiritual teacher Anthony de Mello tells the story of the master who claimed that a major reason for unhappiness in the world is the secret pleasure people take in being miserable.

The story goes that a friend said to his wife, "Why don't you get away and have a good time, sweetheart?"

"Now, dear one, you know perfectly well that I never enjoy a good time!" was her annoyed reply.

There are people who do not open themselves up to new experiences, to adventure, and to opportunities for growth. They choose to remain closed, holding on to their own narrow perspectives and opinions no matter how erroneous or fallacious. Not only do they miss the potential and possibility waiting to be discovered in those precious 86,400 seconds but they also waste that time.

De Mello relates another wonderful story that illustrates such a person:

A woman was walking down a street and suddenly stops a man, saying, "Henry, I am so happy to see you after all these years. Dear, you have changed so. I remember you as being very tall, and you seem so much shorter now. And you used to have a pale complexion, but it is so ruddy now. How you have changed in five years!"

The man finally spoke up and said, "But my name isn't Henry."

The woman calmly responded, "Oh, so you changed your name, too!"

No matter what the reality may be, some people cannot accept another view. Narrow-mindedly, they go through life with blinders and are simply unwilling to take on another perspective. I know we cannot please everyone. Even God can't do that! But we can make choices to find the gifts in each of our precious seconds every day, to look for opportunities of growth and possibility that will stretch us and broaden the circle of our relationships. We can find the blessings and joy, the sacred and the sacrament, that fill so many of our seconds. We can truly live and celebrate each and every one of them.

We can be people who believe in ourselves, appreciating the gifts and talents with which we have been blessed. We can choose to be people who are concerned for others and spend some of our precious seconds each day being connected with them, even being responsible for them. All of us can put some energy into our world by acknowledging others and appreciating their gifts and talents. That may mean simply making eye contact and smiling at a stranger, a simple but valuable use of a few of our 86,400 seconds.

2
Smiles
AND BELIEFS

What a difference a smile makes! It can change a mood; it can create a feeling of happiness and fun. When we smile at another person, we send a message of inclusion, an invitation to be part of whatever is happening. We even help our own emotional level when we smile.

James Laird, a professor of psychology at Clark University, conducts research that explores feelings: how they arise, affect behavior, and may be controlled and organized. Laird conducted a study that had participants move their facial muscles in such a way as to create a frown—without calling it that or doing anything else to create a negative attitude. The participants in the study reported feeling angry. When he had the participants move their facial muscles in such a way to replicate a smile, they felt happier and laughed more easily.

Scientists have realized that facial expressions precede feelings and play a role in generating them. If you ask a person to smile, the person soon begins to experience the pleasant feelings associated with that expression. When you smile, you breathe through your nose and exert pressure on the veins in your face, bringing air into your nasal passages that cool the veins and the blood flowing through them. Smiling also changes the direction of the blood flow inside your face, which then causes the temperature of the blood to drop. The cooler blood enters the region of the brain known as the hypothalamus and causes the release of chemicals that can suppress pain and nurture well-being. In essence, smiling instructs our brains to feel good. If you smile, your brain does, too. You feel happier.

People feel lighter after laughing. (Maybe Weight Watchers should include that in their point system!) Studies indicate that when we hear sounds of cheering and laughter, our brains get ready to smile. Even if we fake it, it works! If we *act* happy even if we don't *feel* happy, we end up having a better day. Smiling increases our happiness chemicals. The next time your telephone rings, smile before you answer it even if you don't feel like smiling. By the tone communicated in your voice, the person on the other end will wonder what you've been up to!

Related to choosing to smile is choosing how to view the world and ourselves. All of us have an internal GPS. We are seekers, searching for direction and trying to find our way. We listen to our inner voice and make decisions based on possible choices and internal messages we give ourselves. It would serve us well to listen intently to our inner voice and to be sure we are not holding negative messages. The research indicates that 80 percent of our self-talk (the messages we speak to ourselves in our heads) is negative. This influences our views and perceptions.

When we are unhappy, we find unhappiness everywhere. Recently I heard a fable entitled "The House of a Thousand Mirrors." There was a happy little dog that learned of this abode and decided to visit. When he arrived, he scurried cheerfully up the stairs to the doorway of the house. With his ears lifted high and his tail wagging happily, he looked through the doorway. To his great surprise, he found himself staring at a thousand other happy little dogs with their tails wagging just as fast as his. His smile, stretching from ear to ear, was greeted with a thousand great smiles just as warm and friendly. As he left the house, he thought to himself, "This is a wonderful place. I will come back and visit it often."

In the same village, another little dog who was not happy as was the first one decided to visit the house.

He slowly and laboriously climbed the stairs. With his head hung low, he looked into the door. Reflected back were a thousand unfriendly looking dogs mirroring him. He growled at them and was horrified when a thousand little dogs growled back at him. As he left, he thought to himself, "This is a horrible place, and I will never come back here again."

What we look for, we find. We can be stuck in the negative. We can feel victimized holding onto unpleasant past events or present circumstances. At these times, we are not fully alive. Imprisoned by our own thoughts and feelings, we are inhibited, chained to false perspectives and negative attitudes. We are unable to choose to live fully; we only exist, going through the motions of living. However, if we have no control over the life-*draining* events in our lives, if we simply cannot change them, then we must change our *response* to those events and transform our experience into a life-*giving* one.

At times, our perspective on or our orientation to the world blinds or blocks us. There is a story about a beggar who had been sitting by the side of a road for more than thirty years. One day, a stranger walked by.

"Spare some change?" mumbled the beggar, mechanically holding out his old baseball cap.

"I have nothing to give you," said the stranger. Then he asked, "What are you sitting on?"

"Nothing," replied the beggar. "Just an old box. I have been sitting on it for as long as I can remember."

"Ever looked inside?" asked the stranger.

"No," said the beggar. "What's the point? There's nothing in there."

"Have a look inside," insisted the stranger.

The beggar managed to pry open the lid of the box. Struck with disbelief and astonishment, he saw that the box was filled with gold.

Our minds are powerful things. More than one hundred thousand chemical reactions go on in our brains every second. Scientists tell us that we have been blessed with natural happiness-enhancing drugs. These drugs are just waiting to be released to every organ and cell in our bodies. Endorphins are the brain's painkiller. They are three times stronger than morphine. Dopamine promotes alertness and a feeling of enjoyment. Serotonin calms anxiety and relieves depression. We are a walking drug store!

We have the power as well as the possibility to increase our level of happiness and joy. Studies indicate that everyday activities such as gardening, listening to relaxing music, stroking a pet, smiling, singing, and enjoying a hug will increase our happiness level. Psychologist and pioneer researcher in the field of empirical happiness measurement and intervention Dr. Michael Fordyce showed that simply focusing attention on becoming happier can have a powerful effect. In his research examining happiness as an applied science, Fordyce demonstrated that students who asked to study the habits of happy people actually increased their happiness and life satisfaction just by learning about the subject. When we are with happy people, we feel happier ourselves. When you are with someone who is positive, you light up; your eyes reflect life, your face softens, and you look and feel good!

Dr. Arthur Stone, distinguished professor and director of the Applied Behavioral Medicine Research Institute at Stony Brook University, found that pleasant events, such as having dinner with friends, gave a boost to the immune system that lasted for two to three days. The same study indicated that a stressful encounter, such as an argument with your spouse, slightly depressed the immune system for just one day. Not only do positive events more than compensate for the negative ones but also it would benefit our health to increase the ordinary pleasures in our day. The absence of these easily accessible choices may take a greater toll on our health than stress.

One way to increase the ordinary pleasures in our day is to increase the time we spend with other people. The human connection is so important. We were created to be social beings; we need people in our lives, and we need healthy relationships. We walk together through our spiritual lifelong journey. We need to care for others and have others care for us.

Researchers have discovered a fascinating phenomenon that validates the importance of human connections: if you perform an act of goodwill and altruism toward another person, such as holding a door open for someone or assisting an elderly person across the street, it will give your immune system a boost. Even more interesting is that someone simply witnessing the event will also get a boost. We are influenced by each other's actions; simply being part of someone else's good mood elevates our own mood and spirit.

Simply sharing a bit of laughter with another person increases our health as well as theirs. It is a form of communication that brings us closer to another. Laughter is a metaphor for the entire range of positive emotions: hope, love, faith, cheerfulness, humor, creativity, playfulness, and confidence. How rich is one who has a laughing buddy!

3
Other People
TOUCH US

Can you remember when we didn't have cell phones? It's hard to imagine how we managed without them. Cell phones are now a part of our world. They even seem like a part of one's anatomy as people walk around with them attached to their ear or as an appendage to their waist, hanging off a belt clip. There was a time when seeing someone walk down the street talking to themselves would elicit pity or compassion for that person. Sometimes we would even judge the person as the victim of a mental illness. That judgment has been transformed as we have grown into a culture that talks incessantly, twenty-four hours a day,

seven days a week, to "someone." What was once a hand-held device is now disguised through Bluetooth technology. We are now part of everyone's conversation: we overhear business exchanges and corporate negotiations, listen as parents reprimand children to accomplish required tasks and assist with household responsibilities, and hear expressions of love and affection once reserved for intimate settings or private venues. Is it easier and perhaps safer for us to speak through a phone because we do not see the person? The depth of communication is diminished because we miss facial expressions and gestures when communicating by phone, through e-mail, or by texting. On the phone, the message is conveyed only through tone of voice and choice of words. Once we hang up, we can only judge from limited communication; we have no idea how we have left the other person, upset or happy.

Words are as important as the messenger and the way the message is communicated. There is a lovely story of an aunt who went to visit her five-year-old niece. The aunt lived on the opposite coast of the country so she planned a month-long visit to be able to connect with her family members. She especially wanted to spend time with her niece. They had weekly phone calls, and Aunt Jenny would listen to Katie giggle as she told funny stories. Jenny wanted to be present to Katie; she wanted to spend some quality time with her. She wanted to take her out shopping, go to a movie, and do special things to create some wonderful memories together.

Every night during her visit, Jenny had the treat of tucking Katie into bed and reading her a good-night story. Each night Katie would request the same story, "Cinderella." After a few weeks of reading the story and being unable to persuade Katie to fall asleep listening to a different story, Jenny came up with what she thought was an ingenious idea. She decided to record the story so Katie could listen to it when she went to bed and fell asleep. Jenny figured it could even be used after she returned home.

The first two nights it worked like a charm. She would go up to Katie's room, give her a big hug and kiss, wish her "happy dreams," and start the recording of "Cinderella." Jenny would then leave and Katie would listen to her aunt Jenny's voice narrate her favorite story as she dozed off to sleep.

The third night, however, Katie said she didn't want to listen to the recorded story. She wanted Jenny to read to her. Jenny was happy to oblige.

That night Jenny brought up a few books so Katie would be able to make a choice of another story. However, Katie didn't want any of them. She wanted to hear "Cinderella" again!

Jenny was perplexed. Why? Katie had the story on tape. She knew every word of it. Was there a reason she only wanted "Cinderella"? Didn't she like the recording?

"Katie, you can listen to 'Cinderella' on the recording I made for you; I narrated the whole story for you. You can listen to it anytime you want."

"I know, Aunt Jenny. But it's not the same. When you read me the story, you play with my hair while you're reading. And when you get to the part about the shoe, you tickle my toes. I just like it so much more when you read it to me aloud."

There is so much more to our communication besides words. These nuanced gestures and subtle touches create the connection we have with each other. These nonverbal messages offer a sense of safety and security, as well as intimacy and love. That connection communicates a sense of belonging.

All of us need an Aunt Jenny. We all need those intimate, tender touches in addition to words. Messages that say, "You're important" and "I care about you." Isn't it strange that no matter how many times Katie heard the story of "Cinderella," the message was different when Aunt Jenny read it aloud to her?

Virginia Satir, American author and psychotherapist, reminds us that we need four hugs a day for survival, eight hugs a day for maintenance, and twelve hugs a day for growth. Wouldn't our day be lighter and happier if we spent a few moments enriching our life and the lives of others by being in the moment, honoring the present, and being free enough to choose growth? I bet we would see more smiles. I would wager that communication with each other would be richer and people would talk directly to one another, rather than only through cell phones or text messaging. We would pay more attention to the things in front of us and live each second aware of the blessings that are ours in the moment. We would create memories to hold in our hearts that sustain us through difficult times. And we would embrace each second that is given to us, living fully.

4
Hopes
AND DREAMS

We all have dreams: things for which we yearn or wish. We have unrealized ideas, places we wish we could visit, people we hope to one day meet, dreams from childhood that remain unfulfilled, or desires and goals that we dream of accomplishing or achieving. Some of us are lucky enough to be able to cross some of these dreams off our "bucket list"; we realized specific hoped-for desires or experienced particular dreamed-of events. But for all of us, this list of dreams and hopes continues to grow throughout our life. Some of these desires are given a voice and become real; others remain silent desires in our hearts.

I have always wanted to be a tennis champ. I wanted to win the Grand Slam: the French, the Australian, Wimbledon, and the US Open. I imagined my name in lights as I dreamed about being "No. 1" in the tennis world. Even as I have grown older, I have never lost my love for tennis or my desire to achieve greatness as a tennis player. Now, of course, I know it is not possible, but we don't have to let dreams die.

In 1957, Althea Gibson won Wimbledon. She was the first African American woman to achieve this. I remember watching the match on television. Glued to the TV set, I imagined my dream of becoming a tennis star as real. I have visited the US Open in Flushing, New York, several times. My love for the game grew as I watched Billie Jean King, Martina Navratilova, and Chrissy Evert play out my desire. Yes, Jimmy Connors, Björn Borg, Ivan Lendl, John McEnroe, Andre Agassi, and Pete Sampras (and the list goes on) were also inspirational, but my heart always returned to the women's matches. After all, that's where my name would appear!

Whenever possible, I would watch every match played at Wimbledon. Even after having followed every match and known the outcome, the first thing I would do every morning is check the newspaper for the sports news so I could read the tennis reviews and check the scores. For years, I would watch the Centre Court matches at Wimbledon and think to myself, "Someday, I will see that court."

It happened! While in London, Patti and I found our way to Wimbledon. Even though there weren't any matches being played, the experience of being inside that venue was thrilling. I sat on Centre Court. I sat on No. 1 Court. I followed the same steps each of these tennis masters walk to enter the stadium, the same hallway that leads to Centre Court. I stood on the concrete edge of the grass courts that are so carefully groomed and perfectly manicured. Different from the clay courts of the French Open or the hard surface of the US Open, these grass courts of Wimbledon are reseeded and trimmed regularly to maintain an exact height of eight millimeters, roughly about the length of your pinky fingernail! No one is allowed to touch the grass, and you may very well be hauled off by security for even thinking about taking a blade of grass home as a souvenir.

I didn't need a blade of grass. My dream had become a reality. I was at Wimbledon. I saw the billboards that listed the champions, and I walked the corridor that exhibited photos of all the Wimbledon champs. I snapped a photo of Althea Gibson's display as well as several other tennis heroes. I sat in the spectator seats on Centre Court and saw every detail that I had only previously been able to view on television. I quietly thought about how dreams come true. True, my dream was not fulfilled completely as I had desired. No, I will never be a Wimbledon champion, but I did get to Wimbledon. I sat directly across from the Royal Box situated at Centre Court. I breathed the same air as the champions. You may never see my name in lights as a Wimbledon champ, but I did. And that was enough for me!

Dreams are not always impossible realities. Sometimes our dreams and desires may be more realistic. For example, perhaps we dream of spending more time with those we love. Sometimes our dreams are as practical as hoping for a few hours to do nothing or to just read a book or to take a nap. But even these more realistic or practical dreams are ways to focus on who we are, what we need, and even what we want.

We need to dream and to desire. How sad when we "know" things will never materialize or become a reality. When (or how) did we cultivate such cynicism? Why are we so afraid to hope? Past disappointments may prevent us from dreaming. Perhaps we don't want to be so vulnerable again, opening ourselves up to more frustration with unfulfilled hopes and desires. But parts of dreams can come true. Bits of hope can become reality. Gifts wrapped in small packages come into our lives giving hope and offering possibility.

Make a list of dreams and hopes. But first, give yourself the freedom to go wild while writing this list. Don't evaluate your dreams as you write them, judging the level of possibility or improbability. Don't clip the wings of your dreams before they take flight. Don't hold yourself back. Too often we close our mind and heart to potential, to what might happen or occur. Give your dreams a voice.

This is not living in a make-believe world. It is not childish or immature to have dreams. It is what keeps us going; it is what gives us hope. It is what opens us to opportunities and encourages us to risk doing things we would never think possible.

5
Gifts
AND TALENTS

Many times we hold ourselves back because we just don't believe in ourselves. We can't affirm our own gifts, don't trust our capabilities, or can't acknowledge our accomplishments, so we remain stuck or just apathetic. Some even let others define them so they never stretch to discover who they really are or reach their own potential.

There is a great story that illustrates this for us. There once was a hiker who found an eagle's egg high on a mountain. Not knowing what kind of egg it was, he carried the egg down to the prairie and placed it in the pen next to a prairie chicken.

The eaglet hatched with the brood of prairie chicks and grew up with them. All his life, the little eagle, thinking he was a prairie chicken, did what his fellow prairie chickens did. He scratched in the dirt for seeds and insects to eat. He clucked and cackled as they did, and he flew no more than a few feet off the ground.

One day, the young eagle saw a magnificent bird flying high above in the cloudless prairie sky. The majestic creature gracefully glided across the sky propelled only by an occasional flap of its powerful wings.

"What a beautiful bird!" the young eagle said to one of his prairie chicken brothers.

"That's an eagle, the king of birds," clucked his companion. "But don't get any ideas. You can never be like him." The young eagle never gave it another thought, and he lived his life close to the ground, thinking he was a prairie chicken, never daring to soar.

Some of us are content to be defined by others, like the eaglet confined as a prairie chicken; others need to dream big and soar higher to fulfill what they know is innately theirs. The choice is ours to recognize our own potential and believe in ourselves. It isn't always easy, but the result is fantastically fulfilling. In risking and stretching ourselves, we discover our own gifts, talents, and abilities. We open ourselves up to new experiences and grow in confidence.

Sometimes it takes another person to help us to find our personal gifts. At other times it takes a challenge from a confidant to help us risk that discovery. That's why it is so important to remember how connected we are and to nurture relationships. When we help others grow into who they really are, we, too, discover new dimensions about ourselves. It has a ripple effect. The seed gets planted and the flower begins to grow. Henry James once said, "A teacher affects eternity; he can never tell where his influence stops."

There is a great story about a good piano player who was part of a trio performing at a bar. People came to the bar just to hear him play. One evening, one of the nightly attendants at the bar told the piano player that he didn't want to hear him just play the piano anymore. He wanted to hear him sing a song as well.

The player said he didn't sing. He was a piano player and not a singer. But the customer was persistent. He told the bartender, "I'm tired of listening to the piano. I want that guy to sing."

The bartender told the piano player that, if he wanted to get paid, he'd sing a song for the patron. This was a faithful patron and the bartender didn't want to lose his business.

The piano player had never sung in public before. He felt he had no choice if he wanted to be paid. So, for the very first time ever, he sang while he played the piano. No one had ever heard the song "Sweet Lorraine" sung the way it was sung that night by this piano player, Nat King Cole.

He had unrealized talent. He may have lived the rest of his life as a piano player in a bar had he not been forced to sing that evening. Nat King Cole went on to become one of the best-known entertainers in America.

We cannot allow our fears to define us. If we do, we may never know what is possible. "Never be afraid to try something new. Remember, amateurs built the ark; professionals built the *Titanic*." Perhaps this message would be a wise maxim on which to hold.

The eaglet believed the prairie chicken and never discovered its potential. Nat King Cole was challenged to discover a gift of which he was not aware. We all have hidden talents. How will we ever know what ours are if we don't risk and try something new or different? Antoine de Saint-Exupéry writes, "A rock pile ceases to be a rock pile the moment a single man contemplates it, bearing within him the image of a cathedral."

6
Sacred
MOMENTS

It is important that we believe in ourselves and develop a positive self-concept. Life is a series of steps toward growth. We constantly become aware of new things about ourselves; we are never too old to discover new things about and within us. As we look back we often remember how we have changed. Some things develop as we grow into maturity; other insights may occur as we age and grow in wisdom and grace.

It is impossible to view goodness outside of us if we do not see it within us. We must begin with ourselves and recognize our own blessings and talents.

Anthony de Mello relates this point in the classic dialogue between a spiritual master and a novice disciple:

"Why is everyone here so happy except me?" asked the novice.

"Because they have learned to see goodness and beauty everywhere," the spiritual master replied.

"Why don't I see goodness and beauty everywhere?"

"Because you cannot see outside of you what you fail to see inside."

We learn a bit more about ourselves daily as we interact with others, as we stay open in prayer, and as we look at the choices we make in relationship to the people who touch our lives. We must be responsible for growing into our full potential. That's the path to wholeness. The Indian mystic and yogi of the nineteenth century, Ramakrishna, suggests, "The winds of grace are always blowing, but you have to raise the sail." In the Jewish Talmud, we read, "When you die, God will hold you responsible for all the gifts you have been given that you did not enjoy."

So often we remain blind. We not only miss internal realities but also do not recognize external gifts showered upon us from unlikely people and places: sunsets, smiles, and compliments that enhance who and *how* we are. We miss unexpected surprises and things that could tickle our hearts and make our souls soar. We fail to see the gifts that come our way in things such as a surprise phone call or a handwritten note wishing us well or expressing the fact that someone is thinking of us. We ignore the blessing of reconnecting with an old friend or an unanticipated encounter in a grocery store with someone we worked with years ago. Our eyes remain closed to the fact that we are blessed with moments of joy and happiness throughout our day. We become numb and oblivious, taking life and all that it entails for granted.

Often, we miss the obvious as if going through life with our eyes closed. The Talmud asks the question, "If not now, when?" If we don't live our lives now to the fullest, when will we ever have the chance? If we don't pay attention to the little astonishments of life right now, right this second, when will we be able to? We need to live each day with wide-eyed wonder, aware of the moments and people around us.

I was once traveling to Sacramento, California. On the connection from Chicago, the plane was full to capacity. I had an aisle seat, and next to me in the middle seat was a young African American man. Through the majority of the flight, he had the tray table down from the seat in front of him and used it as a headrest to sleep.

At one point during the flight, he woke up, turned to me, and asked, "Do you know how much longer before we get to Sacramento?" I looked at my watch and tried to calculate the time. "One hour and forty-five minutes I replied." He then put his head back down on the tray table.

I realized that I had calculated the time based on the wrong time zone, so I quickly said, "You have to add another hour to that. I was figuring out the time based on Chicago time and my watch is still on New York time."

He sat up and said, "You from New York?"

"Yes. I'm from upstate New York."

"What does that mean?"

"I'm from Albany, New York."

"Oh." He then continued, "I'm from . . . I lived in Atlanta, Georgia, but now I am moving back to Sacramento. My brother was murdered, and I have to go home for my mother."

"I am so sorry. I will pray for you and your mom and your brother, too."

He then put his head back on the tray table but only briefly. He sat up and looked at me. He wasn't saying anything, but I could see the pain in his eyes.

"How was your brother murdered?"

"I don't know. He was shot in the head. I don't know what happened. Every time I talk to my mother, she cries so hard she can't talk. And I cry, too, so we don't say anything to each other." The man seemed so young and wounded himself. He just sat still and seemed to be waiting for me to continue.

"I'm so sorry."

He then turned in the seat and said, "There was two years' difference in our ages."

I asked him how long ago it had happened.

"Two days ago."

"Oh, you are going home for the funeral."

He just nodded. He didn't have any words to respond. It felt as if they weren't needed anyway.

A few seconds later, he talked about Atlanta, about his trying to find employment, and how now he needed to go home and find a job in Sacramento.

"Do you have any other brothers or sisters?"

"I have one younger brother."

He took a deep breath and sat so very still. Then he looked at me, and it was so evident he wanted to continue talking.

"Do you have any children?"

"No. I am a Sister of St. Joseph."

"Does that mean you are a nun?"

"Yes."

"Oh. What should I do for my mother? How do I meet her?"

I so wanted to hug this young man who was hurting so deeply. I thought how sensitive and caring he was. Despite his pain, he was so worried about his mother.

"Just hug her. Hold her. Let her cry and you cry with her."

He repeated, "Just hug her and let her cry. And I cry with her."

He was silent as he let the words soak in and soothe him. Then he turned and asked, "Cry with her?"

"Yes. She just lost her son. You just lost your brother. When you cry with her, you tell her it is all right to cry. It is a way to be there for each other."

He stared straight ahead, and I heard him say, "Just hug her and cry with her. I can do that. I can do that."

The plane's wheels were touching down as I heard him one more time say, "Just hug her and cry with her."

I looked at him as we were getting off the flight and promised him my prayers. What he doesn't know is how many times I have carried him in my heart; how his desire to be in the moment and comfort his mother despite his own pain has reminded me that spontaneous interactions are sacramental; and how, if we are attentive, unlikely messengers offer sacred moments that surprise and bless us.

A full flight, not an empty seat on board, and I was blessed to sit next to this young gentleman.

7
FINDING *Joy* EVERYWHERE

God puts us where we need to be. We are with the people we are supposed to be with and in the place we are supposed to be. I wonder sometimes why I am standing in front of a certain audience or why I sit next to someone on a plane. Sometimes we catch a glimpse of why certain people touch our lives and why we touch theirs.

I was privileged to be asked to give a retreat about three years ago in Pueblo, Colorado. The church community was a very welcoming group of people, and it was obvious that their faith was the center of their lives. The people shared the bond of community, enjoying interactions and each other's company. It was a very active parish and there was much ownership by the parishioners exemplified through their engagement in the many ministries offered to and through the community.

The first night of a three-day retreat, there was a little girl, Jamie, sitting in the front row of the church reading my book *Tickle Your Soul*. She was totally absorbed in the book and would laugh out loud at certain sections. Needless to say, I was impressed by this six-year-old who seemed to be enjoying lessons of laughter.

I began the retreat, and Jamie never paid any attention to me. She was lost in the book. However, she became distracted by the laughter of the congregation, and I saw her put the book down, look around, and then sit up, crossing her legs on the pew and giving her full attention to what I was saying. I watched as this young girl laughed in appropriate places during my presentation and evidently understood my message.

The second night of the retreat, she was a bit upset because the front row was already full and she had to sit in the second row. However, this did not in any way diminish her attentiveness. At the end of the session, she approached me and told me how much she liked what I had said. She was specific in giving me the details that indicated to me that she paid full attention to the retreat talk.

The third and final night, she had asked her mother to arrive early enough so she could have her front seat back again. Jamie sat up straight and was obviously my best fan in the group. At the end of that session, we were having punch and cookies in the gathering area of the church, and I looked around for Jamie. She was over in a corner crying. I asked her mother what was wrong. Her mother responded, "Jamie is so upset. She is never going to see you again."

Leaving the adult group for a moment, I went over to Jamie. I put my arms around her and told her how special she was. I also told her that the world is small and somehow I was convinced we would see each other again. My message did not seem to console her. Later, while I was talking to some of the others in the room, I noticed she was standing close by. I looked over and she had a piece of paper in her hand. She asked, "Could I write to you?" My response was, "Only if I can write to you." So we exchanged addresses. That began a wonderful three-year relationship that kept us connected through letters. Jamie would write about school, about her mother, and about the many activities in which she was involved. Always she would draw a picture of a heart or a smile or include some special gift she wanted to share with me.

I was invited to return to the parish this past Lent. I happily said I would come. Not only had I enjoyed the community there but I was also excited about being able to see Jamie again. I would be able to keep my promise!

I gave the homily at all the weekend Masses, and when I arrived at the church for one of the Sunday liturgies, a beautiful young nine-year-old walked over to me. Jamie's smile was brighter than ever. What a lovely young woman she had become! We embraced, and I told her how happy I was to see her again. The treat for me came in the form of an invitation to dinner at Jamie's house on Sunday night with her mother and her sister. What a wonderful, unexpected gift for me!

Jamie and her mom came to pick me up on Sunday at 5:00 p.m., and I could feel the happiness shining through Jamie's eyes. They drove me over to their lovely house where dinner was already prepared. They made a wonderful chicken marsala dinner, which they were hoping would be good since it was a new recipe for them. Our conversation was delightful as Jamie and her sister shared stories and their mom filled in so many spaces. I learned that their father had a history of making poor choices. Their mom, raising her two daughters as a single parent, had returned to school and completed her degree. She was now an English teacher. Her children loved to read, and the family shared so many things with me that they did. I saw pictures of a recent trip; I heard about their father and how their mom drove them to see their dad since he was not allowed to leave the state in which he lived; and I heard about their grocery shopping trips each week and how they walked to the store together to save gas, each helping to carry the heavy bags home. It was wonderful to see how this family cared about each other, how they created sacred moments together, and how they valued their family life.

When this retreat was over, Jamie and I said our goodbyes. We hugged a few extra times. I said a prayer in gratitude for this lovely girl who had become so special to me. I didn't promise we would see each other again, but I did say we would keep in touch.

I returned home and sent a thank-you note for the dinner and the evening we had shared together. I told them how privileged I was to have enjoyed their home together with them.

Jamie sent me a letter in response, one of the most affirming letters I have ever received. Many times people will write to me and tell me something about the lecture I gave or a section of one of my books that touched them in a special way. These letters are treasures. Jamie sent a letter that I will always hold dear to my heart. I asked her permission to include her unedited letter here:

Dear Sister Anne,

Happy late Easter. I hope you had a great Easter. My mom, my sister, and I really liked having you over for dinner. Thank you so very much for the card and coming back to Pueblo for a visit. I loved your speeches you gave. The one that really stood out the most to me is when you said "catch the present day and forget the bad things in life and don't let the past drag you down." The reason I thought this stood out the most is because to me you have been the best thing in life I have ever caught and you have made a big difference by making it easier for me to let go of the bad things that have happened in the past and bring in the new and better things. I will remain obtaining good grades in school just for you. Please stay in touch.

Yours truly,

Jamie, your buddy

Not all messages come to us in positive affirming letters such as the one I received from Jamie. Some messages are not quite as clear, and at times we try to search for their meaning.

My eighty-nine-year-old mother fell in January. She broke her right wrist. My mom is an amazing woman with a generous spirit; she is always up for an adventure. Ever positive, she never complains. It was not until the next morning that my sister and I noticed her hand had become twice the size it should be and that her wrist was black and blue. Mom fell in her kitchen and thought she would be fine, so she didn't say anything.

Two weeks later, my sister, who lives with Mom and attends to all her needs as well as those in and around the house—including cooking, cleaning, shoveling snow, cutting grass, and more—fell and broke her left wrist. My sister's break was a bit more serious. She needed an operation in which a plate and screws were inserted to stabilize her wrist. My mom and sister, each with their respective broken wrists, were like two bookends. One with a blue cast on her right wrist and the other with a blue cast on her left wrist, they became very creative in finding ways to manage around the house. When a jar needed to be opened, one would hold the bottom of the jar and the other would unscrew the lid. They say, "Necessity is the mother of invention!" Complementing each other's ability, Mom and my sister Mary Kay managed to adjust to living with one useable hand. Cutting meat was a challenge. One night they were having pork chops, and I asked them how they cut the meat. They told me they were alone and were not concerned about table manners so they each just picked up the pork chop with their good hand and enjoyed it.

These occurrences challenge us to find the meaning in daily events or to understand the reasons things happen. With the help of others, somehow we manage, come through the experience, and even grow and learn from the opportunity. We might even find a bit of joy and laughter in it!

There are other times when people ask us questions
and interact with us, and from very innocent conversations, we grow in friendship with that person. One
of the parishioners in the church community to which
I belong in Albany came up to me on Holy Thursday
evening just before the service began. She asked if she
could ask me a question. "Of course," I replied.

"When does Lent end?"

Not sure I had understood her, I said, "Pardon
me?"

She continued, "When does Lent end? You see, I'll
be honest with you. I gave up wine for Lent, and I am
dying for a glass of wine. When is Lent really over?"

I told her to go home and have a glass of wine. I
knew that's what Jesus would want her to do, especially since it was Holy Thursday, the day Jesus shared
bread and wine as his Body and Blood with his friends.
She asked if I was sure it was over; I assured her that
it was and told her I hoped she enjoyed her glass of
wine.

On entering the church the next day for Good Friday services, I looked for my friend. When I signaled
to her, wanting to know if she enjoyed her glass of
wine, she shook her head no. Then she came over to
me. She couldn't do it. She was taught a long time ago
that Lent ended at noon on Holy Saturday, so she had
to wait until 12:01 p.m. the next day.

On Holy Saturday, I found Janet—by this time I had
learned her name—sitting in a very crowded church

and again I signaled to her, wondering if she enjoyed her glass of wine. Janet nodded and held up two fingers. She had had two glasses of wine. We have had more fun over that simple interaction. But what has been the gift for me is the open exchange we have enjoyed every week now when we see each other. This is how we build community: relaxing together, enjoying each other's company, finding simple little ways to connect or to tease each other, or sharing some funny story together. Through these connections, we nurture relationships; we find joy.

One weekend, I had been away giving a lecture so I wasn't at my home parish. When I returned and attended Mass on the weekend, Janet's friend came to me to say that Janet had had a heart attack. She was in the hospital and had had quadruple bypass surgery. I immediately went over there. It was evident from the smile on her face that she was happy to see me. After she struggled to tell me what had happened, I felt it my duty to inform her that she needed to drink more red wine. After all, we are told that red wine is good for your health, especially the heart! I could tell it was the first time she had laughed in a long time.

I believe in miracles; I believe in the sacred events that unfold in our lives every day. We just don't always recognize them because they are not packaged the way we would like them to be. Or they are not exactly what we are looking for. I believe these miracles come in all shapes and sizes and in all ages: in nine-year-old girls, in eighty-nine-year-old mothers, in our siblings and friends, and even in strangers that pass by us or share a seat on an airplane.

8
Connections

I usually request an aisle seat on an airplane. There is more legroom, and an aisle seat makes it easier to get up and walk around on longer trips. I was surprised to get on the flight to Chicago on my way to San Diego and find that I had seat 10A, a window seat. It was a beautiful day and I thought it might be fun to just gaze out the window. I had my book on my lap and was hoping the person assigned to the seat next to me would see that I was going to read my book and not get involved in a conversation. I have heard enough life stories on planes and in airports. People seem to talk much easier to strangers. They pour out their heart and soul, leaving out very few details of their stories.

The woman assigned to seat 10B arrived with several bags she had to place in the overhead compartment. Juggling her hot cup of coffee with her other items she asked, "Could you just hold my coffee cup while I lift these things into the overhead bin?"

"Of course," I assured her as I reached out for the coffee cup.

While putting her things in the overhead bin and under her seat, she continued her conversation, holding up everyone else trying to board the plane: "You can take a drink of it if you want. I just knew I needed another cup of coffee. I won't talk to you all the way to Chicago. I used to travel a lot, and when I got on a plane I would bury my head in a book so I wouldn't have to talk to anyone." All of this was said in one breath while I held her coffee cup.

Why me? Just a nice quiet ride to Chicago was all I wanted. A few extra minutes to pray. A bit of peace and quiet.

My new friend sat down, took her cup of coffee, and immediately told me she was a knitter. "Do you knit?"

"No," I replied.

"Well, you should take it up. I even teach knitting."

Not wanting to be rude, I asked her if she had read *The Friday Night Knitting Club*. She said she hadn't. I told her it was a great book and that I bet she would enjoy it.

The plane began to take off while my 10B companion tried to convince me of the benefits of knitting. She had published many patterns. She mentioned that once she begins to knit she doesn't talk.

About a half hour into the flight, as she finished her coffee, she reached for her knitting, and it happened: she stopped chattering! She concentrated on her knitting as a meditation, holding the needles and yarn as if sacred.

How important it is for all of us to have something in our lives that we hold sacred. Perhaps more significantly, how important it is for us to recognize the many sacred things that are part of our daily life. We are blessed with so many messages each day, gifted with many people who cross our paths anonymously. Do we hear them, I mean really hear them? Do we see in others' eyes the gratitude they are expressing, the sorrow they are experiencing, or the excitement they are feeling? Do we even take the time to notice or to listen to them?

How can we ever find the joy in front of us if we don't begin to find those sacred moments such as those found by my companion in 10B through knitting needles and yarn? Perhaps what we look for are times that are defined as special, things such as an exceptional party we attend or an evening of entertainment that ends with spectacular fireworks. But really, ordinary moments such as those found through knitting needles and yarn are waiting to be discovered and celebrated throughout our day. Seeing a sunset, listening to the rain, experiencing the joy of childhood, receiving a surprise phone call, reading a note telling you someone is thinking of you, or being the recipient of a thoughtful gesture all announce the sacredness of life and our human need to make it special.

Perhaps we must begin by focusing on moments of gratitude in our life: moments that remind us of the gift of life, of friends, and of family; moments that help us be aware of the blessings in each day and keep us connected to one other; and moments that remind us of those people who touch our lives daily and how easy it is for us not to recognize them as blessings or, worse yet, take them for granted.

More important even than the moments of blessings are those who create the moments that bless us. Sometimes, like my friend in 10B, we learn to make our own times of blessing, but often those times are given to us by others. How do we respond? Blessing and being blessed is reciprocal. It is not only for others to be blessings for us; it is also for us to be blessings for others. We can ease another's burden by listening to shared hurts and concerns. We can make another feel lighter by offering a bit of laughter in his or her day. We extend hope to each other simply by being present. As is the case with my newfound knitting friend, it costs so little to hold a cup of coffee for another or to offer a listening ear.

We are affected by each other. One study on social connections revealed that your degree of social connection predicts not only how many colds you will get but also your odds of surviving cancer. We need others in our life. We need people to talk with, laugh with, cry with, and hug. We need people who care about us and who nurture us so we can believe in ourselves. We need to share our memories with others and build new memories together. Our need to belong and to "be with" connects us physically to each other. Mark Twain says it so well: "The best way to cheer yourself up is to try to cheer somebody else up." Our choice for happiness is influenced by our desire to lift another's spirit. The research reminds us that if we want to be happy, we must make others happy.

9
WHAT WE
Look For

We can increase our happiness chemicals by holding sacred so many of our everyday activities: making or listening to music; planting and working in a garden; experimenting in the kitchen and cooking a meal for and with friends; creating a lovely table setting; walking or stroking your pet; sewing a quilt or mending a sock; and arranging flowers. All of these ordinary tasks, and many more that are particular to your daily life, offer opportunities to foster happiness through an orientation of sacredness.

We need to make a point each day to find these gifted moments. Look for them. You will find what you are looking for. If we look for unhappy people and if we look for negative outcomes, then that is what we will find. It all depends on our choices and how we choose to see the world. What lens will you use?

There is a wonderful story about a tiny village that was beginning to be populated by various groups of people. One morning another crowd came to the entrance of the village. Sitting on the side of the road was a wise old man who was silently observing the newcomers. One of the travelers turned toward the man and questioned him: "Tell me sir. What kind of people am I going to find in the town ahead?"

The wise man responded, "What kind of people were in the town you just left?"

The traveler responded, "Oh, they were terrible people. Always criticizing others. They stole and cheated. Couldn't trust anyone in that town. They never had anything good to say to anyone. No one liked anyone there. I am so glad to be out of that place."

And the wise old man said, "That's just the kind of people you will meet in this town ahead."

Later on in the afternoon, another group of people came to the entrance of the city. One in that group noticed the man sitting on the side of the road. He went over to the old man and asked, "Tell me, what kind of people am I going to meet in that town ahead?"

The wise man questioned, "What kind of people were in the town you just left?"

The traveler's face lit up and he said, "Oh. What fine people they were! Always happy and caring for each other. You felt accepted in every group. People were kind, thoughtful, and considerate. You could trust everyone. I just hated to leave that place."

The wise old man said, "And that's just the kind of people you will meet in the town ahead."

The Greek philosopher Socrates writes, "He who is not contented with what he has would not be contented with what he would like to have." What we look for we find! If we look for joy, peace, and happiness, we will find them. If we look for disappointment, anger, or distrust, we will find it. Perhaps Leo Buscaglia—the American author, motivational speaker, and expert on love and human relationships—says it best: "What we call the secret of happiness in no more than our willingness to choose life." Yes, the mind is a powerful resource. Buddha taught, "With our thoughts we make our world. Think evil thoughts and as surely as the cart follows the ox, evil will follow you. Think good thoughts, and goodness will surely be yours."

10
Believing

There is a wonderful story of a small midwestern town suffering such a terrible drought that nothing was able to grow. Everything was parched and dry. Crops could not grow, animals were dying, and people were suffering.

The ministers of all the churches decided that they would call their congregations together. They announced that all religious dominations would gather the following Sunday at 11:00 a.m. to unite and pray collectively for rain. The people were also instructed to bring something with them symbolic of their faith.

As instructed, the people assembled for this service and brought crosses, rosary beads, pictures of their favorite saints, and favorite holy cards. The ministers had prepared a prayer service, and as the ritual was coming to a close, it began to sprinkle. Then the rain's intensity increased to a downpour. As it rained harder and harder, the people began to cheer, crying out in gratitude for the rain. They were getting soaked with the torrent of water. It was raining so hard that they began standing in mud and in puddles.

There was a nine-year-old girl standing in the middle of the crowd. She held a different symbol from the crosses, rosary beads, and other religious artifacts. She was standing in their midst with an umbrella.

We need to believe and trust. Prayer is always answered. Sometimes it is not the response we are looking or asking for, but it is always answered. Many of the people in the story came together to pray collectively because they were afraid. What would happen if they went much longer without water? Could they survive? How would they be able to grow and sell produce, nourish livestock, and feed their children? Additionally, the community would be under threat from a devastating fire that could destroy and consume houses. The land would be scarred and scorched.

But one in the crowd, a nine-year-old child, was not driven by fear. She brought an umbrella as a symbol of her belief. She trusted that the prayers of all these faithful people would be answered. There was never a question in her mind. This little child was not dominated by fear but determined in faith, trusting and believing that the rain would come. Hence, she was the only one prepared.

We often hold on to fears that prevent us from being prepared to face what is needed. We are caught in the storm of life, adrift without a paddle or an umbrella. Perhaps we have become cynical in our adulthood, forgetting to have the trust of a nine-year-old. Maybe we have let our problems become so overwhelming that our imagination is overshadowed by seriousness and practicality. Others are bored in our company. If life is only about solving problems and addressing issues, we quickly lose the childlike quality to be creative and inventive, to see with eyes of hope and possibility.

We also often beat ourselves up when a situation does not turn out as we thought it should or we are embarrassed because we made what we thought was a stupid mistake! I was on a flight to Kona, Hawaii, and needed to use the rest room. It is no secret that the space in one of those lavatory compartments on a plane is quite limited. The one I was using in the cabin of the plane was unusually small. I pushed what I thought was the lever to flush the toilet. Because there wasn't enough room to see what I was pushing, I just selected the lever closest to my leg. Immediately bells and whistles went off and every flight attendant appeared at the bathroom door. I had pushed the "call button" and from outside the bathroom I heard, "Are you all right?" "Do you need help?" "Can you answer us?"

First I was laughing so hard, and then I was so embarrassed. I tried to reply that I was fine; I just couldn't find the flush button. All of them waited for me to come out of the bathroom. As I opened the door, they cheered. My face was beet red, and we all stood there, laughing uproariously. Now I have learned to identify where the flush button is before I use the toilet; I don't need to alert any future flight attendants of my basic needs! As embarrassing as this was, though, I didn't berate myself for my mistake. Sometimes we just need to lighten up, believe in our own goodness, and laugh at ourselves.

11
Living IN THE *Moment*

Friends are blessings in our lives, nurturing our souls. Being in their company conjures up feelings similar to listening to a magnificent piece of music or experiencing the beauty of a fragrant garden filled with beautiful flowers. Friends have a way of transporting you, transcending the moment. Suspended in time with them, you feel as if nothing happened before or after; all that is real is now, and you are present to one another in the moment.

My garden of friends has a person who has enriched my life for so many years. Rose Ann is probably one of the most generous, kind, selfless, hospitable,

and funny persons I have ever known. She finds a
way to connect all the people in her life so we are all
aware of others' adventures and activities. For the last
eight years, Rose Ann has been living with ALS, also
known as Lou Gehrig's disease. She has been confined
to a wheelchair that she named Ramblin' Rosie. This
wheelchair allows Rose Ann to be with us whether
we are sitting at her kitchen table, in her living room,
or on the deck in her beautiful backyard. Her "talking
computer" allows her to share her thoughts, feelings,
concerns, and stories. Her web TV affords all of us the
opportunity to communicate with her daily.

Last summer, all of Rose Ann's children and their
spouses, her grandchildren, her best friend, Renee,
and I spent several days together at Chesapeake Bay.
The home was right on the water, and the house had
been constructed by a man who had been diagnosed
with ALS. Hence, the design of the house was totally
accessible; everything and everyone was within reach
for Rose Ann and she was to us. Her grandchildren
are charming. They range from ten months to eleven
years old and have more energy than a football stadium filled with eager fans. However, they also believe
I come to the summer vacation spot solely to play with
them. "Here comes Anne! Here comes Anne!" they
scream as I walk in the door. I suppose when they get
older they will realize I go to be with my friend Rose
Ann. I thoroughly enjoy Rose Ann's children as well.
I hold special memories of babysitting for them and

accompanying them on family vacations each summer to Cape Cod in Massachusetts. But last summer, they were thinking that I had come to Chesapeake Bay only to play with the grandchildren, too!

Three-year-old Jonathan takes my time. His smile lights up a room and steals your heart. I saw him sitting on the sofa and asked him just to sit there for another second while I took his picture. I have a Canon 35-millimeter camera that I operate manually, setting the f-stops and shutter speeds depending upon the speed of the film, the light, and the context of the photo.

Jonathan sat patiently while I took a few shoots and then he said, "Let me see it, Anne!" I must have looked puzzled because he repeated, "Let me see it!"

Realizing he thought I was shooting with a digital camera, I said, "No, Jonathan. It's not that kind of camera."

"Yes, Anne. Let me see it. It's on the back, Anne. It's on the back."

I turned my cameral around so Jonathan could see that the back of my camera had no LCD screen. He just looked. It was a look of, "She must be dumb. There's supposed to be a picture on the back."

Three photos later he asked for the last time to see the picture "on the back, Anne." Then he threw up his hands and walked away. This three-year-old only knows the digital world. He had never been exposed to a 35-millimeter camera before. I can't wait until he grows up and I can tell him this story. I'm not sure how his reaction will change.

We are sometimes like Jonathan, limited by our environment and what we have learned from it; we are shaped by our experience, only aware of what we see and what is in our surroundings. We don't know there are other ways of doing things or seeing things. The lens through which we view the world can be narrow and incomplete. We hesitate to try new things or to investigate if there is another way of doing something because we feel secure with what is familiar. Often, we fall into predictable behaviors and patterns, doing the same old thing the same old way. Hence, limited by our own vision, we forfeit "stretching" opportunities and broadening experiences that might provide a "wide-angle view" as well as new ways to interpret the world and to explore "what ifs" or "I wonders."

Jonathan's world (in cameras) is only digital: click it, view it, file it, or delete it. Even he, at three years old, can shoot photos. However, the photo world for him does not include black-and-white photography. He does not know what a "dark room" is in terms of photo developing or the process involved. He has never heard of photo-processing techniques such as dodging and burning. His world is point-and-shoot. As a three-year-old, his cultural experience has been shaped by digital technology. A 35-millimeter camera is an unknown cultural artifact from the past.

Aren't we grateful when others open our world to new experiences? Were you ever invited to someone's house for dinner and served an entrée you had never had before? Most of us were raised with strict instructions to eat whatever is served and to be polite when you are a guest in someone's home. Do you remember being surprised by the experience and actually liking this new food? Like Jonathan being introduced to a nondigital camera, often it is through other people that we are introduced to new ways of viewing the world.

Recently, I was on a flight from Baltimore to Albany. The flight attendant was a bubbly woman who obviously loved her job. Cheerfully, she served our sodas and juice. As she handed people the beverage of their choice, she made a personal comment to each. I witnessed the smiles and the fun everyone experienced.

Later in our trip, the flight attendant announced that she was dimming the cabin lights. "I'm going to turn off the cabin lights and ask all of you to look out the left side of the plane. You will see a beautiful sunset. We have the opportunity of seeing this so often and many of you do not. So as I turn the lights off, please look to the left side of the plane."

Everyone obediently looked to the left and was treated to this outstanding beautiful gift: a sunset above the clouds. The view was spectacular. The chorus of "ohs," "ahs," and other expressions of awe confirmed how touched everyone was by this beautiful scene. What if the flight attendant hadn't drawn our attention to this treat for our eyes? What if she never turned the cabin lights off and asked us to look out the left side of the plane? What a gift we would have missed! Many of us would have been too busy reading our books or catching a few minutes' nap or being engrossed in a DVD to have gazed out the window to witness a scene that obviously touched everyone deeply.

The flight attendant gave us time to absorb this sunset and then told us she was coming through the cabin to pick up our plastic and paper products. She sang a four-verse parody of "Coming 'Round the Mountain." Her words, however, were "Comin' through the Aisles to Pick Up Trash." Her beautiful singing had the whole plane clapping and keeping the beat. She then proceeded through the cabin and disposed of the trash. But her job wasn't complete!

Returning to the microphone, she informed us that we had a soccer team on board who had just won the game they had travelled to play. She talked about how wonderful it is for kids today to be involved in sports and other productive activities. After praising them sufficiently, she asked all of us to affirm them by applauding. Again, the whole plane responded.

Then she pointed out that there were many people on board who serve in the armed forces. She said that many were dressed in uniform but there were some in civilian dress as well; the attendants knew who they were because they have a roster of names. On behalf of all of us, she voiced gratitude for their service and assured them of our continued prayers. She then sang the most beautiful rendition of "God Bless America" I have ever heard. There wasn't a dry eye on the flight. Just as she was completing her patriotic acknowledgment, we touched down and the plane landed.

Leaving the plane, I stopped to thank her for making the trip so enjoyable and for all of her efforts in making it so special: pointing out the beautiful sunset, acknowledging the soccer team, applauding the armed service personnel, and the touching rendition of "God Bless America." She had made everyone feel as if he or she were the only passenger on the flight. It was obvious she enjoyed her work. For me it was so evident that she had learned to seize every moment and see the beauty and joy present in those moments. She didn't just keep these moments to herself, though; she knew how to share them with others and challenge them to live in the moment, too! What a gift!

12

Laughter

So often we sit back and just expect things to happen. We expect and wait for phone calls from people we want to hear from. We feel we should never have to wait in lines in grocery stores. We assume all drivers are polite and courteous.

There's a story about a man who wanted to win the lottery. He knew it could change his life and he would be able to give his family many material possessions that were needed but that he could not afford. So he prayed, "Dear God, let me win the lottery!" Each day, he would pray that same prayer: "Dear God, let me win the lottery!"

As the days and months rolled by, he became more frustrated and would pray in a louder voice, "Dear

God, let me win the lottery!" After about six months, he got down on his knees, folded his hands in prayer, looked upward toward heaven, and in desperation yelled, "Dear God, please let me win the lottery. If I could win the lottery, I can take care of my family."

And from heaven he heard the response, "It would be helpful if you bought a lottery ticket."

We have to do our part. We need to be responsible, proactive people. Wishing for things doesn't make them real. But what makes life easier is when we engage with others and share time with them, even if it's in the grocery store checkout line! When we share life and spend time enjoying the company of others, frequently we find the gift of laughter. How often when we sit around telling stories and sharing memories do our tales result in uproarious laughter? There is an unstoppable energy that laughter provides, especially when one story generates another. We really don't get tired when we are laughing. It is a gift we give ourselves and others. How often have you sat around a table with good friends, enjoying good food and good fellowship, and engaging in one funny story after another when you suddenly realize how late it is and how long you have been around that table? Laughter and humor keep our spirits alive. Laughter is like a ray of sunshine; it brightens our day and lightens our lives.

Laughter is also like a magnet; we tend to gravitate toward people who are laughing. We want to be part of the group and connected to those who are exercising their bodies and energizing their spirit with this wonderful gift. Laughter forms bonds and creates relationships because we feel closer to people when we can relax with them, trust them, and laugh with them. Relationships shaped by humor are usually the more meaningful relationships in our lives. Hence, we want to spend more time with these people. It's always a joy; it never feels like hard work. Laughter gifts us with the kind of bond that creates instant friendship. These friendships are sustained for years. There is a social aspect to laughter, and it is something done best when shared with others.

Several studies have shown that laughter is good for our health. When we laugh, our blood pressure falls, and blood and oxygen flow more easily through our coronary arteries; our autonomous nervous system returns to a better balance, and our immune cells become more active against viruses and cancer. Laughter also has a calming effect on us. It elicits inner peace and joy. When you laugh, your brain releases endorphins, the body's natural painkillers, which produce sensations of pleasure. Imagine how differently you would feel if you laughed the next time a driver cut you off or sat idly after the traffic signal had turned green. Imagine how you could convert stress to pleasure!

I believe one of the blessings of laughter is that it allows us to see we are more alike than different.

Laughter brings us together; it unites us. Think for a moment: every one of us has tripped and then looked around to see if anyone else saw us trip; we have all walked into a room looking for our glasses or car keys and then forgotten why we walked into the room. Sharing things such as these and laughing at ourselves gives others permission to laugh at themselves. In these superficially stupid moments, human nature becomes our bond. Our differences dissipate; our similarities deepen.

It's all about being actively involved in living and making connections with people, even in seemingly unconnected places. When we cherish each moment, we find joy and laughter. We build healthy relationships. We enhance our own mental and physical health. We become united *through* our humanity.

One of my closest friends has been diagnosed with Alzheimer's disease. Janet and I entered the Sisters of St. Joseph on the very same day back in 1961 and have been dear friends ever since. Throughout the years, we have maintained our relationship during visits at holiday times or when both of us were attending the same meeting. Some years our face-to-face encounters were less frequent, but our strong bond of friendship never weakened. Janet held many positions within our community, including being part of the congregational leadership team on the national level. Additionally, she was registrar of the College of Saint Rose in Albany for many years. Of her many accomplishments and myriad ministries in service to God's people, none was held more dearly in her heart than the decades she spent at our missions in South America living among and serving the people of Peru.

Janet had been in Peru for twenty years when she began to show signs of confusion and forgetfulness. She knew something was wrong and would confide in me. Finally, after addressing concerns from the sisters with whom she lived and after consulting with medical professionals both here and in Peru, it was decided she needed to return home. However, she would need assistance for the return trip. I was asked to go to Peru to accompany her home. It was simultaneously a profound privilege as well as a deeply painful experience to travel to Peru that last time. While I had made the trip several times during Janet's tenure there, this time I was going to bring my friend home. I knew she was not well, and something told me she would never return to the land and the people she loved so deeply.

I spent a week in Peru, helping to pack Janet's things. Each day, however, when I left the room, she would unpack everything, not understanding why they were packed in the first place. Janet didn't want to leave, and her impending departure was filled with so much sadness for all of us. Janet loved Peru. She loved the people and her ministry with them. She was working with poor peasant women, enabling them to learn skills that would lead to empowerment; she loved preparing young children for the sacraments, helping them to know the God of the poor. Janet loved our sisters in Peru. One of the greatest blessings I have received in my many visits is to share community with them. Each visit brought a deeper experience of communion.

The reality of Janet leaving this place she loved so much permeated the week-long preparations for departure. Our hearts were heavy with feelings of sadness, sorrow, loss, and disappointment. Many moments brought tears to our eyes as we watched her forget simple tasks such as how to put toothpaste on her toothbrush and saw her confusion over what to do with it once it was on the toothbrush. We were careful to monitor her actions, being sure she turned off the burners on the stove and did not leave the house unaccompanied, or wander off alone during the night when sleep escaped her.

What helped us all get through this week were moments of release, when the feelings of sadness were temporarily suspended and our spirits were lightened a bit with humor as we found something that made us laugh. Looking for her missing passport became one of those moments. We searched everywhere: in every drawer and through every pocket in slacks, skirts, and sweaters. Knowing we needed to find the passport so

she could leave the country, I suggested we pray to
St. Anthony. St. Anthony always finds missing things!
(Now I'm starting to imitate the man with the lottery
ticket!) I said, "We need to pray 'Tony, Tony come
around. Something's lost and must be found.'"

I taught the other sisters this prayer. Now, accompanying the search throughout the house for the missing passport was the sisters' mantra, "Tony, Tony come
around. Something's lost and must be found." There
was even a cultural interpretation of my prayer. From
one of the rooms I could hear Sister Inez deciding to
do her own variation. As I walked into the room, I saw
her looking upward with hands clasped together in
prayer, chanting "Antonio! Antonio!" As a loyal saint,
St. Anthony heard our prayer, and we found the passport. Of course, we did keep searching while praying!

Recently, Janet suffered a seizure and became hospitalized. She remained in the hospital for three days.
I would arrive at the hospital before 8:00 a.m. each
morning. The first morning that she was more cognizant of her surroundings, I walked into her hospital
room to find her still in bed with her breakfast tray on
the table untouched.

Using the nickname I gave her on the first day
we met due to her predilection for desserts, I said,
"Sweets, you have to eat. If you don't eat, you won't be
able to leave the hospital. And if you don't eat, you'll
lose weight and get thin. Then I'll have to go on a diet
and lose weight." My friend, who says very little these

days and hardly ever utters a whole sentence, looked at me and said, "Fat chance!" What else could I do but laugh? Not only did that get me through this very difficult time but also it got Sweets to eat her breakfast.

13
THE *Lighter* SIDE

Are you familiar with the story regarding the potato farmer who failed to pay his income tax? He was placed in jail. But his wife and children were also suffering.

The wife wrote him a letter telling him how upset she was. "How can we get along without you now? It's almost time to plant the potatoes, and there is no way I can plow the field by myself," she wrote.

Her husband wrote back to her. "Don't plow the field; don't dare touch it. That's where I buried the money."

Several days later, his wife wrote to him again. "You dummy! Don't you know they read the mail in jail? Yesterday the sheriff, the FBI, and the IRS were here digging up that whole field searching for the money. Now what am I supposed to do?"

Her husband responded, "Now's the time to plant the potatoes. Now's the time."

We all enjoy it when we can get one over on someone else. This story certainly had a positive outcome as the prisoner outwitted the authorities while at the same time assisting his family.

We need to help ourselves see the lighter side of life. We need to learn to relax and laugh, to celebrate and enjoy ourselves. Sharing embarrassing moments is one of the best ways to learn not to take ourselves so seriously. Recall my story about pulling the wrong lever in the airplane bathroom. In my book *Tickle Your Soul*, I wrote about falling off the plane and losing the heels off my shoes. And some may recall my story of my priest friend who stutters. One morning at a staff meeting, he mistakenly opened the door to the bathroom, which I was occupying, and exclaimed, "J-J-J-Jesus, C-C-C-Christ!" "Not quite," I said, "Come in or get out, but close the door!" The next day he thanked me for not embarrassing him. Why would he be embarrassed? I was the one on the toilet!

It is helpful to attempt to laugh at situations rather than to bemoan or regret them, only seeing the negative side. When we look for the humor in a bad situation, we uncover the irony and absurdity of life. This is cause for great laughter!

It is helpful to surround ourselves with reminders to help us to lighten up. Put up a funny poster in your workspace. Keep a toy on your desk. Frame photos of you enjoying time with family and friends. Choose a computer screen that makes you laugh or smile every time you see it.

Deal with the stress in your life. If you don't, it will deal with you. Stress blocks us from seeing the humor in our day. We need to keep things in perspective. Many of life's daily happenings are beyond our control. Additionally, we have no power over another's behaviors. Don't rent space in your head for things like that. People are going to act the way they want to act, not the way you want them to act. You only have control over your own behavior.

Watch children play and try to be like them. Children's play is their work; they are experts at play. They use play to figure out the world and its meaning. Children take life exactly as it is; they treat it lightly. They laugh a lot and exhibit great joy. They fantasize and they create; they play pretend and fashion reality. Imagine if we could approach the world with such lightness of spirit. This is not to imply an irresponsible frivolity but to suggest a healthy balance for what is truly important in the grand scheme of things.

Learn to take some deep breaths and practice patience. "There was a time," the story goes, "when, if a person missed a stagecoach, it was not a problem. They just waited for the next one to come through town six months later. In the fast-paced world in which we now live, people have a breakdown if they miss one section of a revolving door."

Sometimes we need to have some space and privacy. Sometimes we need to give that gift to others. In one story, that gift is known as the "Italian Secret to a Long Marriage."

There is a weekly husbands' marriage seminar at St. Peter's Catholic Church in Toronto, Canada. At one of the sessions, the priest asked Arnoldo, who was approaching his fiftieth wedding anniversary, to take a few minutes to share some insight regarding how he had managed to stay married to the same woman for all these years.

Arnoldo replied to the assembled husbands, "Well, I've tried to treat her nice; I spend the money on her. But best of all is, I took her to Italy for the twenty-fifth anniversary!"

The priest responded, "Arnoldo, you are an amazing inspiration to all the husbands here! Please tell us what you are planning for your wife for the fiftieth anniversary."

Arnoldo replied, "I'm gonna go pick her up."

14
Surprises

I belong to a wonderful worshiping community in Albany, the parish of Mater Christi. There I have found a faith community to which I feel connected. Before and after liturgy, you hear people asking about each other, promising prayers for family members, arranging luncheon dates, and sharing stories about children and grandchildren. When a family member is hospitalized, the care and concern passes quickly throughout the community, and one can be assured of cards, visits, and prayers for that person.

As a member of a worshiping community, one has the responsibility and the privilege to minister in different capacities. I am always honored and humbled as I serve as a eucharistic minister. It is an awesome experience to be the Christ-bearer: the person who offers the Body or the Blood of Christ to another. To witness the faith in the eyes of the recipients is a profound experience.

A few weeks ago as I stood at my assigned position, the people processed down the aisle two by two toward the front of the church. As they are offered the Eucharist with a simple reminder, "Body of Christ," they smile and respond, "Amen." But far more is communicated at that moment; the communion goes deeper. A connection between the one giving the host and the one receiving the gift is an unspoken moment of gratitude. Between us we share a belief, and in that exchange, we are connected.

One Sunday during the communion procession, a woman was standing in front of me wearing a red sweatshirt and red sweatpants. Her hands were folded at her waist. As I held up the host, she reached out her hands to accept it. Without the support of her hands, her sweatpants immediately slipped down to her ankles. Realizing what had happened, the woman declared in disbelief, "Would you believe it? Would you believe it?"

Those next to her and those two or three behind her in line could see what had happened. The fervent facial expressions immediately gave way to broad smiles. The woman again looked at me and asked, "But would you believe it?" I tried to console her, telling her it was all right. It seemed forever before she bent over and pulled up her sweatpants. Giving her the host, I simply said, "It's really okay. The day will get better."

Several people who witnessed this were smiling and quietly laughing. In fact, it took a few minutes for all of us to compose ourselves. I am sure, however, that this unexpected moment that caught us by surprise was as sacred as those moments in which we sat quietly and reverently with eyes closed and heads bowed in fervent meditation.

Things such as this happen. Perhaps they are gifts from our God, reminding us not to take ourselves so seriously. Perhaps they are reminders to see the surprise, joy, energy, and goodness in each moment of our life. Perhaps they are moments of grace offered to connect us through laughter.

On my way out of the church that morning, an elderly woman walking slowly in front of me turned around, looked at me, and smiled as she said, "Would you believe it?"

We shared another moment of laughter. We were not laughing *at* the woman in the red sweatsuit. We were enjoying the unexpected moment of an awkward surprise. The smiles and embraces for the woman were messages of support, understanding, and an attempt to ease her embarrassment.

These things are beyond our control as are so many events during the day. The best-made plans are often turned upside down: a quick trip to the grocery store where we encounter long lines at the checkout counter, others making demands on us and interrupting our plans, rain on our family picnic, or detours on roads, to name a few. It is not what happens to us that matters but rather how we respond that can make all the difference. We can hold on to stress, embarrassment, and frustration, or we can try to find a way to cope with it and keep it in perspective. We hold the power to make a choice for a positive response to the event.

15
Perspective

According to a study conducted recently, we are told that we are going to spend three years of our lives waiting in lines. Knowing that, how do we spend those minutes? Are we frustrated and do we complain? Are we annoyed because someone in front of us at the grocery store has a hundred coupons to get twenty-five cents off a loaf of bread? Do we incessantly honk our car horn thinking we can move the traffic faster? Do we hang up the telephone because we have been on hold for too long?

We all know that we have choices. When we choose to live in the moment fully and not buy into the frustration and anxiety of the situation, we often find that our choice to remain positive offers us a few moments

of respite and relief. We begin to see anew and open our eyes to different opportunities. Our perspective changes and offers us new insights. We become more open to what is really happening and often find a solution that previously seemed elusive to address the situation.

Recently, I was taking an early flight out of Albany to New York and then to Phoenix, Arizona. Waiting at the designated gate, I heard an announcement being made from across the hall: "May I have your attention for one moment? I need to stop the boarding process and make the following announcement. We have a problem on the flight. There is a piece of equipment on the plane that is not working correctly. We have a choice. We can all sit here in Albany and wait for the mechanics to come and replace the piece, resulting in at least a two-hour delay, or we can board the plane and go to New York without hot coffee service. The piece that needs to be replaced is for the coffee pot. Cold drinks will be served once on route."

The passengers all jumped up and began boarding the plane. The groans and complaints that were audible when the announcement was first made were replaced with cheers and smiles accompanied with comments about not wanting hot coffee anyway!

How our perspective changes when we listen to the full message and not just hear part of it! Not only are our ears affected but also our feelings and thoughts. There are consequences even to our physical well-being. When the message is negative, it causes erratic patterns that have a damaging effect on our bodies. When we feel sad, frustrated, or angry, stress hormones and cholesterol are released into the body. Our heart pumps faster, causing blood pressure to rise. This can blur our vision, limiting us from seeing the whole picture, literally!

How often have we had small but meaningful experiences that we let slip away as insignificant? Maybe we have had a marvelous conversation with a friend, sat in a warm house wrapped in an afghan or in a cuddly sweater on a cold, bitter day, or laughed until our faces hurt and tears rolled down our checks as we shared some precious moments with another. In our everyday interactions and events, we are blessed with countless opportunities that remind us of the joy and happiness available and accessible right before us. These awesome gifts are epiphany moments calling us to be grateful people. Each of us has the ability to focus on happiness and to choose joy. This is not dependent on some external force; we hold the power within us even when we are simply waiting. Whether in our world, neighborhood, family, relationships, work situation, or when we are alone, we can find joy and positive energy in the moment. But it will depend on our attitudes and our personal choices.

The following story illustrates this so well:

One day, an old woman walked up to a dusty building site where three strong, young men were working hard laying bricks.

She walked up to the first man and asked him what he was doing.

He replied rather rudely, "Can't you see? I'm laying bricks. This is what I do all day long—I just lay bricks."

She then asked the second man what he was doing.

He replied, "I'm a bricklayer and I'm doing my work. I like to take pride in my craft, and I'm happy that what I do can feed my family."

As she walked up to the third man, she could see that his eyes reflected pride and accomplishment. His demeanor was pleasant; his countenance, joy filled.

She posed the same question to him, and he replied with great enthusiasm, "Oh, I'm building the most beautiful cathedral in the whole world."

16
THE
Present Moment

Delays are difficult. You try to make a plane connection, hurry to get off one plane, run to your connecting flight at another gate, and then you wait. Some days you sit and watch the monitor. This reminds me of the day I was supposed to connect to a flight in New York City that was departing for Albany at 9:20 a.m. I had just traveled from Phoenix, Arizona, and had taken the red-eye so I could be home for most of Saturday. The monitor indicated that the 9:20 flight was departing at 10:10 a.m.; then it changed to 10:20 a.m. The ten-minute delays continued up to an 11:55 a.m. departure time. I didn't want to look at the monitor again because each time I glanced at it, there was another delay.

Waiting is a part of life. We wait excitedly for planes. We wait impatiently for stoplights. We wait expectantly for people who are coming to celebrate special days with us. We wait anxiously for a certain piece of mail to arrive. We wait hopefully for a baby to be born. We wait patiently as we sit beside a telephone for that call from a special person.

We wait as we watch the seasons change. The warm, humid summer nights fade gently into autumn's crisp, cool beauty. Then we wait and watch the season slip away as fallen foliage is replaced with a beautiful blanket of wintry white. Again we wait through the long winter for the surprise of spring with buds poking through the last remnants of snow. Now the earth is covered in the beauty of colorful and fragrant crocuses, daffodils, and tulips announcing new life.

There is a plethora of emotion; the wide range of feelings extends from excitement to frustration as we wait. When it is a happy, positive experience, the wait can seem endless as your heart races with anticipation. When it is a sad experience, the wait can seem heavy and burdensome.

Sometimes the only way to ease the interminable waiting and bring lightness to the moment is to connect with another person. Talk to someone. Even a stranger will do. Voice your frustration, fear, or anger. As we hear ourselves giving voice to our feelings, we may then begin to release the inner tension created by those overbearing feelings. Our muscles relax; the strain in our body eases.

What we look for we find. Our perceptions shape our interpretations of things and people. When we attend a concert and expect it to be uplifting and entertaining, that's what we experience. It we go to a meeting and dread going, anticipating that it will be a waste of time, that's the way the meeting goes.

A God seeker came to the rabbi and said to him, "I'll give you a kopeck if you can tell me where God lives!"

The rabbi answered him, "And I'll give you a hundred kopecks if you can tell me where God doesn't live."

When you are sad, you find sadness. When you feel happy, you find things that produce happiness. Our expectations shape our awareness. We see what we expect to see. Our experience is fulfilled through our expectation. If we expect to be miserable while we wait, we will be. If we choose to share the burden of waiting with another, though, we might be able to produce happiness for ourselves. If we look for God, we will find him.

17

MAKING
the Best of Things

Last summer, I traveled to Greece with Patti who was presenting a research paper at an international conference on early childhood music education. We travel well together; it's easy, and we always have a wonderfully relaxed time sharing the adventure. I was particularly excited about this trip. I had been to Greece many years ago, but I didn't have anyone with whom to share the experience of visiting such sacred sites. I was happy to be with her on this trip. Our first week was in Corfu; the second week of the conference was held in Thessaloniki. The beauty of Greece awakens your heart. The Aegean Sea surrounded us with peace

and tranquility as we breathed in the ocean air; it was a deeply spiritual experience. Walking in the footsteps of St. Paul and having the Acts of the Apostles revealed in such a real, beautiful, and unique way brought the presence of these holy people into the moment. When we were in Philippi, I could hear Paul say, "I thank my God every time I remember you, constantly praying with joy in every one of my prayers for all of you." As I stood by the stream where Paul baptized Lydia, the first woman to be christened, and saw where he was imprisoned and persecuted with Timothy, I realized that I would never hear the Acts of the Apostles the same way again. My respect for Paul grew by leaps and bounds. I admittedly always thought of Paul as arrogant and chauvinistic. However, the acts of baptizing the first woman and enduring his prison sentence have given me a whole new perspective on him.

As life giving, relaxing, and informative as this trip was, it also had its challenges. There were moments where we had to adjust and be creative. Travel today is not easy. Planes are filled to capacity, resulting in overcrowded and tight conditions. One often feels victimized by the airlines.

Patti and I began our trip at the Albany Airport with a flight to Philadelphia where we were to connect to a direct flight to Athens, Greece. Our 11:20 a.m. flight from Albany was cancelled at the last minute because the flight attendant was not feeling well. The clerk at the ticket counter assured us that it would be no problem to make our connecting flight, which was departing from Philadelphia at 4:20 p.m. Our new departure time from Albany was now 2:00 p.m. As the time approached, the board indicated the departure time had changed yet again. Now the delayed flight would leave at 3:00 p.m. Again, we were assured that there was "no problem" making our connecting flight in Philadelphia; it was only a forty-minute flight and we would have plenty of time. Our 3:00 p.m. flight left Albany at 3:30 p.m., and needless to say, our 4:15 p.m. arrival prohibited us from making our 4:20 p.m. connection.

The customer service representative offered us several options, rerouting us via Munich, Paris, or Rome to Athens. We settled on Rome since we could get assigned seats rather than fly "standby," which was the case if we chose another flight. I wasn't leaving the country without a guaranteed seat! Because of the delay in Albany, we missed our connecting flight from Athens to Corfu, resulting in another five-hour wait in Athens. Once in Corfu, we watched as one piece of luggage after another tumbled onto the conveyor belt, but ours was not among them. The Aegean Airline representative was as helpful as she could be. However, thirty-six hours after departing Albany, we left the airport in Corfu and headed toward our hotel with nothing but the clothes on our backs. Arriving at the hotel Sunday evening, we realized that this particular European hotel did not have the same amenities as those to which we were accustomed to in the United States: there was no toothpaste or toothbrush, but we were grateful for shampoo and soap. We would have to go to the market in the morning to get the items we needed. It opened at 8:00 a.m.

Making the best of the situation, we both washed out our underwear and hoped it would be dry in the morning. We used the towels for pajamas (probably more information than you need!). Patti was giving her presentation on Monday morning, so she had to present her paper in the clothes that she wore since departing from Albany. Each day, I would call the airline to no avail; we were not getting any positive information regarding the location of our luggage.

Finally, our luggage arrived on Wednesday at midnight. We were just returning from an evening of Greek food, music, and dance organized by the conference host. As conference participants departed the bus and entered the lobby of the hotel, the concierge announced, "We have luggage!" Everyone cheered for us. Some even took pictures of us gleefully standing by our luggage. Truly, this was a historical occasion! We had luggage, which meant that we had clothes and we had toiletries. It is amazing how one can improvise and do without a lot of things that we think we need; it is equally amazing how much we appreciate these things we so often overlook after having to do without them.

The airline saga continued, however; there's more to the story! We were now departing a week later from Thessalonike to Athens, making our connection to Philadelphia and from Philadelphia to Albany. As we approached the ticket counter, the airline attendant assured us that she would check our luggage straight through to Albany with no problem. However, shortly into processing our tickets, her expression changed; we knew something was wrong. The airline had cancelled our reservations because of the changes made to our initial flights. We had no return tickets! The ticket agent sent us back to the Aegean Airline counter since that was the airline on which we were supposed to travel back to Athens. The woman there told us that there was nothing she could do because it was the weekend; this issue couldn't be resolved until Monday or Tuesday. We nicely tried to work with her, pleading for her to help us. In the meantime, I also called back to the States to my travel agent and woke her up; it was midnight in Albany, but we were desperate. We needed tickets for a departure!

Yes, we did leave Greece that morning, and interestingly, we were on the same flights and in the same seats that had originally been booked in our names. Travel can be a hassle. Under the circumstances, we stayed as positive and polite as we could, and with the assistance of many people, our efforts were rewarded. Both of us took a deep breath when we finally boarded the airplane and were comfortably settled in our reserved seats. We did get home and with only a twenty-minute late arrival into Albany!

18
POOR *and* RICH

I was resting on a bench in a lovely park across the street from the hotel in which Patti and I were staying in Corfu, Greece, for the week of Patti's conference. It was a beautiful place to sit, reflect, pray, and enjoy some quiet time while Patti was in the morning session of her conference. I was breathing in the air of the Aegean Sea as I enjoyed the flowers and delighted in the various shades of green in the park. A woman was sharing the park bench beside me. She was smoking a cigarette and enjoying a hot cup of coffee. Being from New York, I was a little taken aback as the smoke drifted in my direction. It is rare to see someone smoking in a public space in America since smoking

is banned in restaurants, parks, and all public areas. This ban is strictly enforced.

Our conversation began very simply with a comment on how beautiful the day was and how bad smoking is for you. Without hesitation, the woman began to tell me her story. This woman was homeless and was spending these few moments getting ready to face the day. She could not find work anyplace, so when the opportunity to clean a bar room every morning presented itself, she quickly grabbed it. Certainly it was not enough money on which to live; she couldn't pay her rent, but she explained that a friend was letting her stay at his house free of charge. She wasn't worried about eating because she had planted tomatoes, cucumbers, lettuce, and a few other vegetables in his backyard. She convinced me that she had plenty to eat each day.

After cleaning the bar, she would treat herself to one cup of coffee. She found a place where it only cost one Euro, a bargain. Each morning, she would drink her coffee on this park bench and plan where she could go to apply for a job. Every day she searched. She wasn't fussy, and she would take any work that she could get. She conveyed no negative attitude throughout our conversation. Her attitude seemed to be, "it is what it is"; if life hands you lemons, make lemonade! She had accepted the circumstances of her life. She seemed neither hopeless nor discouraged. This was simply the way life was and the conditions with which she had to deal. She was convinced that her difficulty with finding employment was due to age discrimination, not effort. She did not let this stop her; relentlessly she kept applying for one position after another. (My guess is that she was in her thirties, but she felt that employers were hiring very young, attractive women and she was "too old.")

She openly talked about her mother and the concerns her mother had for her. Her mom lived in Athens, which made it impossible for them to visit often. While she was inviting me into her world, several people passed us as they walked their dogs in the park. She then began to speak of her animals. She had just found two disabled kittens: one was blind; the other, deaf. She was nursing them back to health. She would use her earnings to buy some medicine and rub their eyes. It made her smile to see the kittens improving and getting stronger; her happiness was its own reward. The kittens were all she had. The woman added that she would regularly find stray animals, nurse them back to health, and then find a home for them. It occurred to me that she was reaching out and doing just what she needed others to do for her. She needed to have someone nurture her and bring her to health and then find some security and safety in the world.

For an hour and a half we talked about what it was like for people to struggle in this world and how we are responsible for each other. "People need to be there for each other," she told me. She talked about violence, how it gets played out in our lives, and how destructive it is to everyone around us. I didn't do a lot of talking; I just listened as she told me her story and revealed so much about her life to me. I thought to myself that this woman seemed poor and rich at the same time. Despite her inability to find work, she was caring, sensitive, intelligent, and hopeful, and she desired to live life fully.

19

BEING *Different* ISN'T SO BAD

Not long ago I was told a wonderful story that happened to be true. In August 1939, Bob May finished a story he had been asked by the department store Montgomery Ward to write for Christmas, a story that would be distributed to every child who came to visit Santa Claus at the store that Christmas. A month before, his wife, Evelyn, had died of cancer. His four-year-old daughter, Barbara, was distraught over the loss of her mother and couldn't understand why this had happened; Bob was depressed and brokenhearted.

Growing up, life had always been different and even difficult for Bob. As a young boy, he was often

the brunt of bullying at school due to his short height and slight stature. He was different and just didn't seem to fit in, so he became the focus of malice and name-calling. Although his childhood had been difficult and the loss of his wife was devastating, Bob was blessed to have his little girl and was grateful for his job as a copywriter at Montgomery Ward during the Great Depression. So when Montgomery Ward asked him to write a Christmas story, Bob tested it out on Barbara: it was a story of a little reindeer that didn't fit in. Thus was born *Rudolph, the Red-Nosed Reindeer*. No one expected the story to be a hit, but in 1946, seven years after the story was first distributed, Montgomery Ward printed the story in book form and distributed more than six million copies of the children's tale.

The next year, Montgomery Ward gave Bob the rights to Rudolph, a much-appreciated gift as the cost of caring for his wife during her illness had left him deeply in debt. When Johnny Marks, Bob's brother-in-law, wrote a song about Rudolph that was recorded by Gene Autry in 1949, Rudolph's popularity soared, and the song was second only to "White Christmas" for the most Christmas records sold. Though he continued to work, Bob's financial future was secured by a reindeer with a glowing red nose, a reindeer based in part on his own past. Perhaps this story communicates that being different isn't so bad. In the case of Bob May, it was a blessing.

All of us at times feel we don't fit in, we don't belong. Get discussions going on politics or religion or even the New York Yankees versus the Boston Red Sox and "differences" are made manifest. Treat yourself by sitting in the middle of a crowded shopping mall and witness the differences in dress, the way people walk, the actions and expressions of young children, or the way older couples support each other, holding up their spouse over and over again. All of these examples honor differences and celebrate diversity.

Why do we judge differences undesirably and view them through a negative lens? Why not interpret differences and the various dimensions of our day as a large flower garden beautifully adorned with a multifaceted array of vibrant and varied colors? Interpreted through this lens, we create a beautiful picture to behold and to celebrate.

Judgments so often limit us. We get into black-and-white thinking with narrow vision. We don't see the goodness and the blessings that are present. Judgments get us stuck. They diminish creativity and limit options as possibility pales. We become close-minded, and our vision is blindsided from potential.

What a grace it is to stay open to others even if we don't agree, to see another way of being, and to hear another way of interpreting the world around us. How surprised we might be to hear a message that could have gone unheard because of preconceived judgments.

20
Judgments

I was listening to two people sitting in the booth next to me at a restaurant discussing their friends. There were so many judgments, and both documented examples to justify what they were saying. I was hoping my own luncheon companion would arrive so I had someone with whom to talk and wouldn't be paying attention to this conversation. One friend in particular that they were talking about didn't do anything right. She always said the wrong thing and used the wrong words. She dressed inappropriately and wore colors that did not flatter her. Her hair wasn't tinted properly, and even her shade of fingernail polish was dull.

I wish I could have met the woman they were talking about so I could see if I had the same impression.

I secretly sat in my booth wondering why they called her a friend. I kept waiting to hear something positive so I could understand why they would even want to spend time with her. It seems to me that, with all those negative traits, it would be far from pleasant just to be with her. I almost wished I could have gotten involved in the conversation. I wanted to share with them a story I had heard recently.

There was a Catholic pastor who had been assigned to two parishes that were both located in Manhattan. He was on his way to the second church one Sunday morning, traveling on the subway. A few stops after he boarded the train, a man entered the same car, and one could not help but look up. The man reeked of alcohol, and his dirty, torn clothes created a terrible odor that began to fill the car. His shoes had holes in them, and the laces were not tied. His pants were torn at both knees. He held a dirty newspaper in his hand. The priest thought it was probably taken out of a garbage can. The man sat quietly on the subway and began reading the paper. After a few stops, the man turned to the priest and asked if he could ask him a question.

The priest said, "Sure."

The man questioned, "How do you get arthritis?"

The priest decided that this was a teachable moment. He was going to say things that hopefully this man would hear and thus transform his life and change his ways.

The priest said, "I'll tell you how you get arthritis. You drink too much. You use drugs. You wear dirty, torn clothes. You don't bathe and take care of your body."

The man just turned away and went back to reading the newspaper. After a few more stops, the priest was feeling a bit guilty and was thinking that he was a bit too harsh on the man. So he decided to reengage him.

"Sir, I'm sorry that you have arthritis."

"Oh, no," the man quickly responded, "I don't have arthritis. I was just reading in the paper that the pope has been diagnosed with arthritis."

Isn't it strange that, through our prejudiced perceptions and judgments and our negative critiques of even the smallest flaws of others, we determine who others are and decide what they need to hear?

21
Meanings

It is so important for us to stay open to new experiences. So many times we get stuck in a rut. We do the same things over and over again as if on automatic pilot. This repetition often causes us to lose the value of what we are doing. Routine can become monotonous. After a while, we don't have to think about what we are doing; we just perform the action mechanically. Boredom and apathy set in, resulting in lack of energy. With robotic motion, we move lethargically from one thing to another, from one action to another.

We need to refocus and reenergize; we must heighten our awareness and generate life-giving moments by seizing opportunities that present themselves to us. Pay attention to the giggle of little

children or the warm eyes of an elderly person. Notice the song of the crickets on a beautiful summer evening or the steady mantra of a spring rain. Hear the hush of your surroundings in a snow-laden landscape or the quiet coo of a baby resting with confidence and contentment in her mother's arms.

Stuck in our ruts, so often we prejudge people, situations, or events, prematurely making up our minds to like or dislike someone or something. Our choices are consequently based on these decisions. We don't try new foods because we know we won't like them. We don't attend a play or movie because "it's not our thing." We don't try a new sport because "we have no interest." We prematurely eliminate possibility, wonder, and surprise.

I love music. I love almost every kind of music. Classical music brings relaxation and healing to my soul. Johnny Mathis, my all-time favorite singer, brings smiles and joy to me with every song he sings. Of course, I know he is singing just to me! The one type of music to which I am not attracted and do not enjoy is country music. I never grew up hearing it and never attended any country music concert. I always viewed it as depressing music: crooners lamenting losses and disappointments with such permeating themes as, "My father left my mother at the mailbox yesterday." Of course, this is a simple example of my self-composed song in country music style. I left out the part about my dog dying!

I was asked to give a retreat day in Bakersfield, California. Two nights before the retreat I received a phone call from a woman inviting me to dinner after the daylong presentation. She wondered if I would be too tired to go out for dinner with a group of people on Saturday night. One of the blessings for me when I give retreats is invitations such as this. It is a time to share stories, relax, and enjoy a meal with others, thereby getting to know the people with whom I had worked on a different level. Because I travel mostly by myself, sharing these moments with others is always a gift to me. So I responded positively to the invitation. My commitment to the retreat would be over, and my flight home was not until the next day.

I was then asked if I knew Buck Owens. I admitted that I had heard of him, but I couldn't recall why his name was familiar to me. My host reminded me that he was a country singer and explained that there was a wonderful restaurant named the Crystal Palace dedicated to the memory of Buck Owens and filled with his memorabilia. Because reservations are required, my host wanted to be sure the invitation would be acceptable to me. Of course! I was grateful for the thoughtfulness as well as the company, and a restaurant based around a country music singer would definitely be a new experience for me!

Tom and Pam, who picked me up in Burbank, would be joining Joi and Larry, the couple responsible for organizing the retreat. They were all excited about having dinner together. Not only was the thought of dinner exciting for them, but the music and dancing all night would be a treat, too! I must admit that I had not shared my very limited knowledge of country music or my ignorance to the experience of line dancing with them.

Joi and Larry drove me to this wonderful restaurant. The parking lot was quite full, so we had to park way in the back. It was obvious that the spot was a popular and favorite venue for the locals. As we exited the van and walked toward the front of the restaurant, Joi shared some interesting information with me: "You know, Bakersfield is known as 'pick-up territory.'"

"Really?"

"Yes," she continued, "It has always been called 'pick-up territory.'"

Listening to her, I wondered why she was sharing this with me. Then I thought how grateful I was for the information and for her care in sharing it with me.

Joi continued, "Just look around."

Now I began looking over my shoulder, around the parking lot. I thought that she was communicating a message for safety, telling me to be on guard: "pick-up territory."

"Look. See." She began pointing to all the pickup trucks in the parking lot. By "pickup" she meant all the trucks!

I said, "Trucks. You're talking about trucks. I thought you were warning me that I needed to be on guard not to be 'picked up'!"

We stood in the parking lot and laughed for several minutes. Both of us were on two different tracks. Everyone in Bakersfield seemed to be driving pickup trucks. That's not my experience being from New York. "Pick up" to New Yorkers has a very different connotation.

This experience made me aware of how our perspective is sometimes limiting and how narrow-minded we can be. I had missed the obvious because it wasn't in my experience or my worldview. How important it is for us to stretch our reality and thereby broaden our perspective. How important it is for us to be open to new ideas, experiences, and other points of view, to view the world with wide-eyed wonder.

As I sat listening to Buck Owens's son, the lead singer for the evening, I tried to "hear" the music differently. I watched couples on the dance floor line dancing, many wearing cowboy hats, all wearing smiles, and all thoroughly enjoying the experience.

Walking into the restaurant, I enjoyed the display of Buck Owens's artifacts. As I made my way through the museum, I read about him and his family and viewed his many and varied guitars and clothing. This wasn't my ordinary world, but it offered me a chance to enter a different experience, to share another's interest, and to learn something new.

No country music will ever replace Johnny Mathis for me, but "pickup" has a new meaning in my vocabulary now. It has made me reflect on how many times during a day I miss the same opportunities. I can miss seeing a beautiful flower bud break through the soil after a long cold winter. Perhaps I may forget to stop long enough to look up at the stars filling the evening sky. Every waking moment offers life-giving opportunities and opens up possibility for new meaning in my life, though not every moment will offer as many new meanings as the one that gave me a new definition of "pickup"!

22
CHECK *Things* OUT

Sometimes friends make suggestions to us, and because we believe in and trust these people, we take their suggestions without questioning them. They make suggestions about where to enjoy a good meal, they recommend a great movie that we should see, they brag about their latest vacation and urge us to go there, or they lend us a book to read that they have enjoyed.

A few years ago, Patti and I were traveling to Rome, Italy, as she was presenting at the early childhood music education conference that had taken us to Greece earlier. The night before we were leaving on the trip, I talked to a good priest friend of mine, Fr. Ken Doyle, who had lived in Rome when he served as the *US Catholic* press correspondent to the Vatican. "Anne, if you don't do another thing when you get to the Vatican, go to the west side and find the elevator that takes you to the top of the dome. There you will see an outstanding view of Rome. Just spectacular!" Believing this was a "must do" for our trip, we made a point to include it in our itinerary.

When we arrived in Rome, we planned a day to spend in and around the Vatican and Vatican City. Even though it wasn't our first trip there, we were still taken by the enormity of St. Peter's Square. As we walked through the basilica, we were mesmerized once again by its beauty and majesty. We paused in awe in front of spectacular art, filled with deep appreciation for the grandeur, the history, and the faith. The aesthetic delight and holy ambiance was a feast for body and soul. We departed from the sacred internal space in search for the elevator at the west side of the Vatican.

We found the location, got on the elevator, and rode up. However, to our surprise, it only took us to a platform that, while not the top of the dome, did offer a lovely view of Rome. To get to the top of the dome, we needed to walk up 320 stairs. There was a warning sign indicating that one should not undertake this endeavor if one had a heart condition or any other kind of medical impairment. Seeing the sign and realizing it was one narrow staircase leading up to the dome and another narrow staircase on the other side for the return trip down, I decided that I didn't want to go on this adventure.

Patti asked, "Why? You don't have a heart condition."

No, I don't, but I am not one who thinks it's fun to walk up a narrow staircase, the steps of which are barely wide enough for one's foot. Additionally, it was a warm July day and the only ventilation was a small window about every hundred stairs! However, I gave in; I didn't want to disappoint Patti, and I didn't want her to go alone. Before long, I realized that as you ascend your body bends to accommodate the curve of the dome while you grasp the railing and struggle to keep your feet steady on the narrow stairs. I said to Patti, "This is definitely not my idea of fun!"

Three hundred twenty steps later, gasping for air, my arms sore from pulling the rest of my body up the stairs and my face fire engine red from the heat, I arrived at the top. I tried to find a bench or a seat on which to rest, but it was obvious that this was a "lookout" level. So I became a leaner, finding a large marble column I befriended until I could somewhat breathe again. Then I fed my soul as I photographed the breathtaking panoramic view. The scene was indeed an exquisite aerial view of all of Rome, and I was happy I hadn't forfeited it! Needing to prove I did this climb, I took several photos from every angle

of what could be seen from atop the dome: the spectacular view of the city, the Vatican gardens, the heralding
angels decorating the perimeter, and the communion
of saints encircling the precipice.

Then I had to face the dreaded return trip down,
which was no easier than the upward climb. The stairs
were as narrow and the air as thin as in the ascent.

Upon returning home, I called my good friend Ken
and told him that not only did I go to the top of the
dome at St. Peter's but also I said some prayers for him
when I reached the top that I could not repeat! Ken
was thrilled we had such a wonderful experience.
"Did you do it, Anne? Good for you. I've never done
it because I am afraid of heights!"

We need to get all the facts before taking a sugges-
tion. Ask questions, and do a bit of homework on your
own. Needless to say, it was a good lesson I learned,
but these are the things of which fun memories are
made, and the retelling of the story makes for good
laughs.

It does not have to be a big event such as the one
I just described to create memorable experiences.
So often it is a small gesture like a smile or a "thank
you" that brightens our day. It may be a compliment,
the sharing of a happy memory, or an unforgettable
tale that brings that smile to our face and warms our
heart. How sad it is that we so often miss these unexpected surprises and unanticipated joys. We get so
busy in our task-oriented days that we lose graced

moments that can make a profound difference in our day and how we choose to use those precious 86,400 seconds.

23
Unexpected
MOMENTS

Benjamin Hoff, in *The Te of Piglet*, relates a wonderful story of a Hindu, a rabbi, and a critic. The three of them were caught by a terrific thunderstorm, and all sought shelter at the same nearby farmhouse.

"The storm will be raging for hours," the farmer told them. "You'd better stay here for the night. The problem is that there's only room enough for two of you. One of you will have to sleep in the barn."

"I'll be the one," said the Hindu. "A little hardship is nothing to me." He went out to the barn.

A few minutes later there was a knock on the door. It was the Hindu. "I'm sorry," he told the others, "but

there is a cow in the barn. According to my religion, cows are sacred, and one must not intrude into their space."

"Don't worry," said the rabbi. "Make yourself comfortable here. I'll go sleep in the barn." He went out to the barn.

A few minutes later, there was a knock on the door. It was the rabbi. "I hate to be a bother," he said, "but there is a pig in the barn. I wouldn't feel comfortable sharing my sleeping quarters with a pig."

"Oh, all right," said the critic. "I'll go sleep in the barn." He went out to the barn.

A few minutes later, there was a knock on the door. It was the cow and the pig.

We all get caught in thunderstorms. Challenges present themselves as we take suggestions from our friends and decide their experiences will be as wonderful for us as they have been for them. Sometimes, we even learn new things about ourselves as we change our perspective and review our assumptions through these experiences.

Recently, I was being treated for a sinus infection. I was instructed to use a certain type of medication, and the doctor asked to see me again in two weeks. My appointment was scheduled for May 3 at 1:30 in the afternoon. On May 1, I received a text message from the doctor's office reminding me that I have an appointment on the third and requesting me to reply to this message to confirm my availability. I do not text. The only text message I have ever sent was to my friend Susan saying, "call me." Now, I was looking at the screen and I thought, "I am really a capable person; I can send a text message back. There is no reason I could not respond to this reminder with a text."

I pressed the "reply" button on my cell-phone screen and proceeded to type my response. I was simply going to write, "I will be there."

I pressed "I" and just as quickly "love you" filled in and went through. Swish! It was gone. I stood talking to my phone as if I could bring the message back. There was my text message out in cyberspace and out of my control, arriving in light speed at my doctor's office. "I love you." Figuring they received a reply and not wanting to cause any more embarrassing communication, I decided just to wait until my appointment to explain.

When I arrived for my scheduled appointment, I walked into the office and was warmly welcomed by many smiles and grins from the staff. It was evident that they had all read my message. I just said, "I need to tell you that I am not here to have an affair or to break up any relationship." I couldn't go any further because the room was filled with such laughter that no one could hear me.

Recently I gave a lecture in Honolulu, Hawaii, at the Big Island Liturgical and Arts Conference. All the presenters were asked to arrive a day early and to stay a day later. This was a wonderful way for the group to get to know each other, and it added to this enjoyable weekend. One of the presenters was David Haas. David is a renowned and talented musician who composes liturgical music and lectures around the country. He is a warm, caring man with a wonderful sense of humor.

As one can imagine, stories were shared over this period of time, and we spent many hours enjoying each other's company. David shared a wonderful true story with me and gave me permission to share it here.

Having had some serious heart surgery the year before, David spent seven days in the hospital and was finally being released. Following discharge protocol, he was transported from his hospital room to the car awaiting him in a wheelchair.

As David arrived at the car, he started to get out of the wheelchair and collapsed. The hospital staff immediately brought him back into the hospital and readmitted him. Anticipating that he was probably going to be there for a few days, he made a request: "If I have to go back into the hospital, could you please get me a movie I can watch. I can't find anything on television, and I am bored to death. Please find me a movie. Any movie."

Desiring to make him as comfortable as possible, the staff searched diligently for a movie but could only find *The Sound of Music*. They brought it to David's room, and even though he had seen it a hundred times and knew every word of every song, it really didn't matter. It was a movie.

At this point of sharing his story with the group, David began to entertain us with the different songs, even imitating the facial expressions of Mother Superior singing "Climb Every Mountain." David recalled how he had collapsed again while watching the movie. He said he had no recollection of what had happened or how much time elapsed. However, as he started to regain consciousness, he could see about thirty people in the room all dressed in hospital clothes holding paddles over him. He wondered where he was and what was happening. Then he heard, "So long, farewell, auf wiedersehen, adieu."

He thought, "Oh, no. I'm dying." The music continued. No one had turned off the movie, and the scene was where the Von Trapp family was leaving the stage to begin their escape! We were laughing hysterically as David told this story. I bet that moment helped his heart, too! We tend to laugh and be more alive in unexpected, surprised moments.

The Sufi Mullah Nasruddin, the ancient Persian folk character who tells stories in the Sufi tradition of Rumi and Hafiz as well as wisdom tales of many faiths, tells the classical joke about the drunk looking for his car keys under a lamppost.

"Where did you lose them?" his friend asks.

"At home," the drunken man replies.

"Then why are you looking here?"

"The light is better."

There are times we are taken "off guard." We hear something differently. The unexpected occurs, and we find ourselves more alive and grounded in the minute. At these times, living fully in the moment, we benefit physically, mentally, emotionally, and spiritually.

Another story with Nasruddin illustrates that same point.

Nasruddin sometimes took people for trips in his boat. One day a fussy pedagogue hired Nasruddin to ferry him across a river. As soon as they were afloat, the scholar asked whether it was going to be rough.

"Don't ask me nothing about it," said Nasruddin.

The scholar was taken aback. "Have you ever studied grammar?" he asked.

"No," answered Nasruddin.

The scholar responded, "In that case, half your life has been wasted."

Nasruddin said nothing. Soon a terrible storm blew up. Nasruddin's boat was filing with water. He leaned toward his companion. "Have you ever learnt to swim?" he asked.

"No," said the pedant.

Nasruddin replied, "In that case, all your life has been wasted for we are sinking."

24

NOT ALWAYS
as It Seems

There is a great story about a lawyer and a senior citizen who were sitting next to each other on a long flight. The lawyer, young and haughty, was thinking that seniors have lost their cognitive capacity; he could get one over on them easily.

So the lawyer asked if the elderly gentleman would like to play a fun game. The senior was tired and just wanted to take a nap, so he declined politely and attempted to fall asleep.

The lawyer, however, tried to get the old man to see that the game could be a lot of fun, so he described it to him. "I'll ask you a question, and if you don't know the

answer, you pay me five dollars. Then, it is your turn to ask me a question, and if I don't know the answer, I will pay you five hundred dollars."

The senior citizen suddenly became interested and decided to play the game. Perhaps then the lawyer would be quiet so he could rest.

The lawyer asked the first question, "What's the distance from the Earth to the moon?"

The senior didn't respond but reached into his pocket, pulled out a five-dollar bill, and gave it to the lawyer.

Now it was the elder's turn. He asked the lawyer, "What goes up a hill with three legs and comes down with four?"

The lawyer immediately used his laptop to browse the Internet in pursuit of the answer. He sent e-mail to his friends. He tried every search engine he could imagine to no avail. After an hour of exploring the Internet, he finally gave up.

He woke the senior citizen and handed him five hundred dollars. The senior placed the money in his pocket and went right back to sleep.

The lawyer went nuts not knowing the answer. He woke up the senior and asked, "Well, so what goes up a hill with three legs and comes down with four?"

The senior reached into his pocket, handed the lawyer five dollars, and went back to sleep.

The lawyer's judgment regarding senior citizens did not hold true. They are not diminished intellectually, slow, or dumb. In fact, be careful if you think you can pull a fast one on them! You see, things aren't always as they appear.

I heard this story about a minister who was walking down the street one sunny afternoon when he noticed a very small boy trying to press a doorbell on a house across the street. The doorbell was too high for the little boy to reach. After watching the little boy's failed attempts, the minister decided to go over and give the youngster a hand. So he crossed the street, went up to the house, and pressed the doorbell with a forceful push.

Bending down to the little boy's level, the minister smiled and asked, "And now what?"

The little boy replied, "Now we run!"

25
OPEN to CHANGE

We often remain closed when our friends' behaviors change. This is especially true when our comrades no longer want to do things to which we have become accustomed or when their interests shift or they develop new hobbies. We, too, may need to change. Or maybe we need to be patient as we try to understand the motivation behind their new choices. These may require a transformation on our part as well as we seek to redefine relationships.

There was a workman in London who went to a pub every evening with his friends and drank away his earnings. As a result, his wife and children were near starvation and living in squalor.

One day, the workman went to a temperance meeting. He stopped drinking and became a churchgoer. His drinking buddies were annoyed at the loss of their friend, so they teased and taunted him mercilessly about his newfound faith in Jesus Christ. One fellow asked him, "Do you really believe that Christ turned water into wine?"

The workman replied, "I don't know about that, but you can come over to my house and see how he turned beer into furniture."

People change, and the labels we put on others don't always hold true either. For many of us, we need help to smooth the rough edges, to alter behaviors, and to change unhealthy patterns. I have had the privilege of working with a third-grade boy during the school year, trying to help him choose more appropriate conduct. He had developed many inappropriate behaviors for getting his own way. If he didn't want to do something, he would throw a temper tantrum and throw himself on the floor, kicking and screaming until others gave into him. Realizing that he was in third grade, one might question why this behavior was allowed to continue. It persisted because he was successful at manipulating others and getting what he wanted. It worked for him.

Each week we would have a session, and based on the feedback from his teacher and principal, we talked about other options of behavior that he might choose. We set very small goals weekly, and over the course of several months, he began to take ownership of the goals. He was realizing some success and even began to be proud of himself. He told me that it was much easier for him when I was in the school. Since I only work at the school two mornings a week, I suggested that he put my picture on his desk!

The child did change and began to look for ways he could handle things differently. The last day of the school year, his mother sent me a beautiful card and wrote a lovely message of appreciation on it for working with her son all year. She noted how much he had changed; she and her husband were proud of the child's accomplishments.

Included in the card was a piece of paper that the student had placed in the envelope. Scribbled on a small piece of paper, the note read:

Dear Sister Anne,
    Thank you for believing in me when I didn't believe in myself. I know I am a better boy than I was in the beginning of the year.

This handwritten note is a keeper for me. How precious that he would write such a sensitive and profound message! He grew in so many ways throughout the year. Always an A student, he continued to excel in his schoolwork. But for me, in addition to academic achievement, he grew into the respectful, dignified person we are all called to be. He looked at himself and his behaviors and worked at becoming an appropriate young man. He took little steps, one at a time. He had setbacks, but we used those setbacks to demonstrate how things could have been handled differently.

This is what we all do: take little steps in becoming more of the person God imagined we could be. While always realizing that we need others for support, we must stay open to what is often right in front of us, transform ordinary moments into sacred ones, and be sure to check out our assumptions and perceptions, the ones we have of ourselves and of others.

26
Guideposts

I was sitting in London, England, where I traveled with Patti. She presented a paper at the international conference Research in Music Education at the University of Exeter, and we set aside a few days to enjoy the sights. I was staring up at the famous clock tower, Big Ben. Not only was I being informed as to the exact time of day but also I was looking at history, a clock recognized for ages as a timekeeper. How many millions of people have looked at this prominent clock? How many have used it as a guidepost to discover their exact location? Perhaps it would be a meeting place or a coordinate for those gathering with others. So much history; so much time!

It is often helpful to look at the past. A Chinese proverb reminds us, "By reviewing the old, we learn the new." We do not review the past to get stuck in it, that is, stuck in the memories, successes, failures, disappointments, or achievements. Rather, it may serve as a guidepost. It is our own history, marking our own time.

The Vietnamese Zen Buddhist Thich Nhat Hanh reminds us, "If you look deeply into the palm of your hand, you will see your parents and all generations of your ancestors." All of them are alive in this moment. Each is present in your body. You are the continuation of each of these people.

We are connected to our past—to our parents, grandparents, great-grandparents, our relatives from several centuries past, to the many saints who have walked the earth, and even to Jesus, to our God. All of these people serve as guideposts, help us see where we come from, and light the passage of time from past to present. It is for us to determine where we will go from here and who we will become. Our past can shape and influence us, but our choices determine who we become.

How humbling to know that as others look into the palm of their hands, they will see us! We, too, are alive in that moment. We, too, are present in their bodies. We, too, are a continuation of each of these people.

Who we are influences all. How we act, what we believe, our dreams, our interests, and even each

breath we take lives on. What an awesome awareness! What a challenging responsibility! Like Big Ben,
we are intersecting coordinates, standing at a cross-
roads, influencing and shaping history, and creating a
past and a future together.

It is for us to determine how we will influence this
moment, finding positive energy and seeing possibil-
ities in front of us. It is for us to make our own lives
whole and holy, to keep that total balance of body,
mind, and spirit.

We can make this moment a happier, healthier time
for ourselves and others. So many little things bring
joy to the moment. There is an old song that was sung
many years ago titled "Little Things Mean a Lot." It is
not in spending money, going into debt, or "buying"
happiness that makes life meaningful. Rather, it is in
giving a bit of ourselves to whatever we are doing and
wherever we are. A simple smile to a stranger, a kind
word to a colleague, a compliment to a coworker, a
note written to a friend, or just a little gesture of rec-
ognition to a relative can bring forth life and foster joy.
There is no price tag for these gifts.

While in London, Patti and I rode on the London
Eye. This structure is the world's tallest cantilevered
observation wheel. It is a huge Ferris wheel that has
walk-in capsules, each holding twenty-five people.
Again, I could view Big Ben, as well as the River
Thames and the highlights of London. While riding
in the capsule, I was taking photos of all the sights. A

small boy about five years old came over to me and asked if I would take his picture. His mother reacted quickly, saying, "Chris, you can't do that." I smiled and said, "Sure he can." As I held up my camera, a gorgeous smile came over this little boy's face. I don't know anything else about him except his name is Chris Jr. But he gifted me, a stranger, with a warm heart and a happy grin, and I have his photo to remember that gift.

I believe we put ourselves in life-giving places. There is a lovely story of a rabbi's child who used to walk alone in the dark woods. At first the rabbi let his son wander off alone. But eventually, the rabbi began to be concerned about his son's safety. The woods, after all, were dangerous. The father didn't know what his son might encounter. The rabbi decided to discuss the matter with his child. One day he took his son aside and said, "You know, I have noticed that each day you walk into the woods. I wonder why you go there."

The boy said, "I go there to find God."

"That is a very good thing," the father responded. "I am very glad that you are searching for God. But, my child, don't you know that God is the same everywhere?"

"Yes," the boy answered, "but I'm not."

We often feel more alive and aware when we are in the presence of certain people or at a place that is filled with memories; these people and places refresh us, instilling feelings of joy, safety, and security. When we feel safe, secure, and happy, and when we find a place where we belong, we tend to return there. In fact, we seek those places out! In these types of stress-free environments, we experience surprises and moments of laughter. Once we choose them, these places and the people who inhabit them become the guideposts that affect our lives and the lives of those who follow after us.

27
LETTING *Go*

I'm sitting by the bedside of my dear friend, Janet. Sitting and watching her slowly transition from this earthly life to her heavenly reward isn't easy. I will miss my friend, but I will be so grateful when this part of her journey is over. She sleeps so much more now; when she opens her eyes, she seems to be seeing all the people who are waiting for her on the other side. I am sure the angels are filling the room and waiting patiently for her to let go and be lifted out of this suffering. While difficult to be companioning her in this process, it is simultaneously an awesome experience to be on this holy ground.

It is very touching, too, to have so many sisters stop by her room. Many stay only a few minutes, but all

go over to her and, tenderly holding her hand, offer words of comfort. Whispering a prayer, they bless their sister and quietly exit the room. The power of community is so evident.

As I sit by her bedside, I talk to her. Still convinced that hearing is the last sense to leave us, I share with her all the news of the day. I find myself recalling some of our wonderful times, and as I recount these memories, I wonder if I am doing this more for myself than for her. I feel so helpless. This stage of dying is such a mystery shaped by so many questions. I find myself asking why. Why does one have to suffer? Why does it all take so long? Why am I even asking why?

Certainly, it will be over for Janet when God finally calls her home. For myself, I am impatient, praying that she will not have to endure this much longer. I have journeyed with her through this terrible disease, Alzheimer's. Many times, she shared her fears and her feelings. Many times, we sat with each other quietly as tears fell softly down our cheeks. What a blessing and privilege this shared friendship has been for me. These days have taught me that we have very little control over life. We really aren't in charge. It is only for us to make choices that help us to live the moments we have, take what is given to us each day, and accept what is happening.

As I sat by her bed the other day, I told her how much I loved her and how I would miss her terribly. I told her what a great friend she had been to me. I assured her that all of us would be okay; she didn't need to hold on for us. But then I told her that it wasn't for me to decide when she would go; everything was in God's time. I was reminded of a story that shared this sentiment:

One day the pastor was visiting his homebound parishioners. He stopped at the home of a very important member of his congregation. He was sure he could hear her moving around inside the house, but she did not answer the door when he knocked. The pastor tried three times, and after no response, he took out his business card and wrote on it "Revelation 3:20" ("Listen! I am standing at the door, knocking"). He dropped the card through the mail slot. The following Sunday after services, the pastor saw his business card in the collection basket. Under the reference to Revelation that he had written was another handwritten message: "Genesis 3:10." He hurried to his bible to find the text. It read, "I heard the sound of you in the garden, and I was afraid, because I was naked."

I guess there is some truth to "timing is everything"! I was unaware of a few sisters who were standing behind me until I heard the laughter. I didn't know others were listening, too.

Not wanting to pass up this tender moment at Janet's bedside, I offered some words of comfort and assurance. Surely God was pleased and would welcome her with open arms saying, "Well done, good and faithful servant." She had lived a life of unwavering commitment to the poor, especially in these last decades ministering with our sisters in Peru. I told her another story, an old legend from Europe first communicated by the Brothers Grimm. I had heard this one many years ago.

Once upon a time, a poor pious peasant died and went to heaven. A very rich man also arrived at the "pearly gates" at the same time. St. Peter came out and warmly welcomed the rich man. Peter led him into heaven and did not even notice the poor peasant who was standing there as well. As soon as the gates shut, rejoicing could be heard coming from inside: music, loud singing, dancing, and laughter. The poor peasant stood listening to this great rejoicing. The frivolity soon ended, and all became very quiet. St. Peter again opened the gates of heaven and ushered in the poor man.

The pitiable peasant was waiting to hear the music, singing, and laughter, but there was none. All was quiet. The peasant turned to St. Peter and said, "I was hoping that heaven would have been different than earth. On earth, the rich are treated with dignity and honor, and given special privileges. The poor are overlooked. So even in God's house the rich are given special treatment." St. Peter walked over to the poor peasant and put his arm around him and said, "Oh no, my dear man. You are just as special as anyone else, and you will enjoy every heavenly delight that the rich man will have and more. You see, poor people such as yourself come to heaven every hour. But a rich man, such as that one, well, they do not come more than once every hundred years!"

As I spend these precious moments with my friend, I have learned that it isn't necessary to fill every second with conversation. At times, it is a precious gift to *be with* each other; the silence—no television, no cell phone, no background music, and even no words—is the blessing. Sometimes we share more in silence than in all of our spoken and heard words. For those of us blessed to have these rare and intimate relationships, the silence speaks volumes and no words are needed because the message has already been communicated.

Years ago, someone sent me an old Japanese story called "The Silk Drum." For me, it illustrates the precious gift of silence.

Once upon a time there lived a mighty lord who realized that his death was very near. He urged his only daughter to marry: "Dearest daughter, your youth is passing and you still have not chosen a husband. All the men who come for your hand you have dismissed. I am going to die without seeing you married and without seeing my grandchildren."

His daughter replied, "No, father, I shall fashion a drum of silk that will be stretched over a bamboo frame. The man who hears the note when my fingers strike the drum is the man I will marry."

The old man thought how foolish this idea was. "A silk drum does not make any sound. I will die without ever seeing my grandchildren." But the daughter had the silk drum made. Many men came to listen to her drum; not a sound did any of them hear when she played her silk drum. Month after month passed, and the many men came to hear the sound, but all went away without hearing it.

One day, a young, handsome, and rich man arrived.

"Where do you come from?" the father asked the stranger.

"From far, far away beyond the seas and mountains," replied the striking stranger.

The father asked, "And for what have you traveled such a great distance?"

"I have come to marry your daughter," he responded.

"My daughter will marry the man who can hear her silk drum. You could not have heard its sound across the mountain and the seas."

"You are correct. No sound of the drum has reached me," the young man admitted.

"Then be on your way like all the others before you. Why do you even linger here?"

"Because I hear its silence," said the young stranger.

And the daughter put away her silken drum because she had no further use for it.

Even in silence, we hear what we need to hear and when we need to hear it. When there aren't any words to offer, we share the silence. That is the message. We give into the silence, and we let go.

Epilogue

PLANT YOUR OWN GARDEN

What if we planted a garden—a garden of vegetables? We would have to prepare the soil, plant the seeds, water them, and nourish and nurture them daily. Each morning we would check the garden for signs of life, waiting patiently to see shoots sprouting through the earth. Once the ground was dotted with touches of green, we would be hopeful and excited that our labor bore fruit, and our hard work was bearing results.

Like a garden, we must prepare, plant, nourish, and nurture the ground of our being. We must be patient with ourselves, watch for signs of new life, grow with

excitement that is borne from a more attentive and conscious orientation toward life and living. We become not only more human but more holy as well.

Let us plant our own daily living garden with these seeds:

Lettuce

Let us be thoughtful of others. Think of another way to do one thing that can create a bit of peace or happiness. Perhaps it will be a simple gesture such as holding a door open for another or taking an elderly neighbor's garbage out. Maybe you check with your neighbor before going to the store to see if he or she needs anything while you are there.

Let us be kind to others. Kindness is a conscious act. You have to decide and choose to act in a certain way. Showing kindness to another may simply be offering a compliment or uttering a blessing for that person. When an act of kindness is performed, one's own heart expands. One feels appreciated and respected.

Let us be alive each moment. There are only so many minutes in each day. Once that moment leaves us, we can never get it back. This very moment has all we need to be alive and to live fully. So often we hold on to yesterday that we forget to live today. Yesterday has no power. It is gone. We can't take a thing back we said. We can't change a thing we did. All we can do is learn from the experience and let it inform future choices, empowering us to decide different behavior the next time. The grace and joy of life is always waiting for us in the present moment.

Peas

Patience. One always wishes for more patience! As we rush around, demanding everything yesterday, waiting can be a real test for us. Every day we wait. In lines at the grocery store, we find ourselves behind someone with several coupons or with a clerk in training as we shift back and forth from foot to foot with frustration; in a traffic jam or at a detour, we feel our blood boiling because of the inconvenience as we watch time click away for an already late appointment. Yet we want to "slow down and smell the roses." Patience means waiting. It means being watchful. Patience means being attentive to what is before us.

Party. We need to have fun, bring people together, enjoy their company, and share their stories. Our culture measures so much by what we do and how much we accomplish. We need to learn to just "be" with each other, to share time and space, life and love. Our societal emphasis on outcomes creates such an imbalance in our life. We need to play and party. We need to create camaraderie and enjoy each other's company. We need to exercise our inner muscles and relax them.

The energy that comes with laughter brings gifts of its own. Hope, bonding, perspective, and a positive attitude are invaluable rewards. Laughing with another bonds us together and touches our hearts; there is nothing that can replace that connectedness.

Perseverance. We are people who want instant gratification; we like immediate success. Scratch-off tickets are purchased by the millions each day with the hope that one can instantaneously strike it rich. When things get too difficult, we easily give up. When something is taking too long, we get impatient and frustrated. But perseverance means we are in it for the long haul. It means staying the course and sticking with it. It offers us a chance to be creative and open to novel approaches to something or someone. There is a wisdom that comes with perseverance. But the awareness of this wisdom is often not seen in the process; the wisdom becomes apparent in the end result.

Turnips

Turn up the ends of your mouth. No other blessing holds the value of a smile given away to another. A smile communicates acknowledgment of and respect for the person with whom it is shared. A smile is a sincere nonverbal message that conveys comfort and connection with another. The benefits of smiling are not just for the recipient, though; they are mutual.

Smiles light up our brains. When we smile, the energy goes back inside of us. This positive energy eliminates negative thinking, which clogs the brain.

Turn things around. Sometimes we feel hopeless. Nothing is going right. Everything you plan seems to be reversed, or your world feels as if it has been turned upside down. But we always have choices. There are always other alternatives in front of us and options that allow us to make other decisions. If your plane has been cancelled and everyone at the airport is yelling and screaming, you can use your energy to look for an alternate flight or to get rebooked. If you plan a picnic, expecting a large number of friends, and it rains on the day of the event, you can be frustrated and angry and cancel the picnic or you can decide to make the best of it and hold an indoor picnic, rent a tent, or throw up a tarp! Thinking creatively, perhaps all you need to do is readjust the time schedule or tweak the menu.

Beans

Be who you really are. You are a gift. You are unique. There is not another human being quite like you. Why try to be someone else? Why not get to like and respect the person you see in the mirror? Why not take care of that person and *be* comfortable with your own gifts? All of us are blessed with unique, special qualities. We even have a few rough spots. Your only constant companion throughout life is yourself. Perhaps the journey of life is the challenge of *being* the real person you were created to be.

· *Be* happy. A while ago there was a popular song that advised, "Don't worry. Be happy." Perhaps the real message was not to worry but to be concerned and responsible and then act ourselves into healthy behaviors. Being happy doesn't imply seeing life through rose-colored glasses. It really means finding the positive message that allows us to have a healthy balance in our daily life. When one experiences happiness, one experiences a sense of peace and well-being. It helps in making the best of all situations in which we find ourselves. Fr. John Powell, the noted Jesuit psychologist and author, reminds us, "Happiness is an inside job." It is an internal quality created by attitudes and beliefs. Attitudes and beliefs are things over which we have control. We can't control events or situations, but we can decide how we will respond to them. I decide if I am happy!

Carrots

Care about yourself. Take one day at a time. Add balance and energy to each day. Make each moment count. Awake with a positive attitude. Look for blessings daily. Create balance—work, play, pray, relax, connect with others, and be sure you have some laughter in each day. Expect surprises each day; your days will gift you with a smile and may even help you to laugh at yourself!

Care about others. It has often been suggested that if you want to be happy, you should make someone else happy. Caring about others means thinking outside of yourself. It is not to the exclusion of taking care of you. Caring for another, however, enriches and empowers who you really are. This care is clothed in many simple acts of kindness: call a friend, send handwritten notes to let people know you are thinking of them, bring a red rose to a friend, or offer an ice-cream sundae to someone you know who loves ice cream. In our age of mass communication, people text, send e-mail, and "friend" each other on Facebook and Twitter. There are endless ways to be able to communicate how we care about others. But it is for us to foster relationships and to respond to each other physically, mentally, and emotionally. Be a "gift giver" to others: give hope, happiness, and joy.

Gardens are filled with a variety of vegetables. Our days are filled with a myriad of experiences. Like the gardener, we must look for ways to enrich our daily growth, seize the moments given to us, and live life to the fullest. Like the gardener, we must cultivate patience, nurture possibility, nourish opportunity, and fertilize each day with life's surprises and ordinary sacredness. If we follow this recipe, we will live well, love much, and laugh often, enriching our lives one day at a time.

Sr. Anne Bryan Smollin, C.S.J.
(1943–2014) was an international lecturer on wellness
and spirituality. An educator and therapist, she earned
a doctorate in counseling psychology from Walden
University in Florida and was executive director of
the Counseling for Laity center in Albany, New York.
Smollin is the author of *Tickle Your Soul* (Sorin Books,
1999), *God Knows You're Stressed* (Sorin Books, 2001),
and *Live, Laugh, and Be Blessed* (Sorin Books, 2006).

AVE

AVE MARIA PRESS

Founded in 1865, Ave Maria Press,
a ministry of the Congregation of
Holy Cross, is a Catholic publishing
company that serves the spiritual and
formative needs of the Church and its
schools, institutions, and ministers;
Christian individuals and families; and
others seeking spiritual nourishment.

For a complete listing of titles from

Ave Maria Press

Sorin Books

Forest of Peace

Christian Classics

visit www.avemariapress.com

AVE MARIA PRESS
Notre Dame, IN
A Ministry of the United States Province of Holy Cross